Conditions for Criticism

CONDITIONS FOR CRITICISM

Authority, Knowledge, and Literature in the Late Nineteenth Century

IAN SMALL

CLARENDON PRESS · OXFORD
1991

Oxford University Press, Walton Street, Oxford OX2 6DP

Oxford New York Toronto
Delhi Bombay Calcutta Madras Karachi
Petaling Jaya Singapore Hong Kong Tokyo
Nairobi Dar es Salaam Cape Town
Melbourne Auckland
and associated companies in
Berlin Ibadan

Oxford is a trade mark of Oxford University Press

Published in the United States
by Oxford University Press, New York

British Library Cataloguing in Publication Data
Small, Ian
Conditions for criticism: authority, knowledge, and
literature in the late nineteenth century.
1. Literature. Criticism, history
I. Title 801.95
ISBN 0-19-812241-1

Library of Congress Cataloging in Publication Data
Small, Ian.
Conditions for criticism: authority, knowledge, and literature in
the late nineteenth century/Ian Small.
Includes bibliographical references and index.
1. Criticism—Great Britain—History—19th century. 2. English
literature—19th century—History and criticism—Theory, etc.
3. Great Britain—Intellectual life—19th century. I. Title.
PR75.S53 1991
801'.95'094109034—dc20 90-47442
ISBN 0-19-812241-1

Typeset by Rowland Phototypesetting Limited
Bury St Edmunds, Suffolk
Printed and bound in
Great Britain by Biddles Limited
Guildford and King's Lynn

TO THE MEMORY OF MY BROTHER
ANTHONY JOHN SMALL
WHO DEPARTED A USEFUL LIFE
28 AUGUST 1989

Quis desiderio sit pudor aut modus
Tam cari capitis?

Preface

A short book on late nineteenth-century criticism which contains two long accounts of changes in the epistemologies underlying nineteenth-century political economy, historiography, sociology, and psychology probably needs some sort of initial explanation. My thesis is that literary critical discourse cannot be properly understood as a phenomenon unrelated to the rest of the contemporary intellectual culture which produced it, one which I test by examining literary critical writing in the last decades of the nineteenth century, but one which I maintain is not by any means limited in its applicability to that period. My argument therefore has two parts to it. First, that there were profound changes in the nature of critical discourse in the final decades of the last century. The general nature of these changes is documented and described in the Introduction. And secondly, that these changes were in themselves related to changes in the nature of *intellectual* authority in all disciplines of knowledge at the time, changes which coincided with the wholesale professionalization and institutionalization of knowledge which took place, principally in the universities. These issues are described in Chapters 2 and 3, and from them I attempt to make some general points about the orientation of disciplines of knowledge in the last decades of the nineteenth century. In these senses, then, I am attempting to describe a sociology of knowledge, albeit in a programmatic, schematized, and skeletal manner. It is my argument that only such a sociology will adequately explain the history of critical writing, and I have used it to analyse, in the second part of the book, the critical writing of two major critics of the time, Walter Pater and Oscar Wilde. I have chosen these two writers partly because I think that the methodology I propose explains their work in a way which is novel, and partly because they can stand as representatives of certain trends in literary culture in the last decades of the nineteenth century. I do not mean to suggest, however, that the conclusions I reach about their work may not be extended to other figures. Indeed I believe that my conclusions have important implications for understanding the work of most writers in the last decades of the last century. I have chosen to restrict myself to two examples simply because my argument stands or falls on general grounds, not on its applicability to a particular writer's. In my final chapter I argue, however, that the type of analysis I use can be fruitfully applied to other periods of literary history—particularly that of the present day—when the role of authority in literary discourse has once again become a vexed one.

Acknowledgements

This book has grown out of a decade and a half of writing and thinking about nineteenth-century literary and art criticism. Many of the ideas and some of the material have been rehearsed in essays for various journals. These in particular are: 'Plato and Pater: Fin-de-Siècle Aesthetics', *British Journal of Aesthetics*, 12 (1972); 'Vernon Lee, Association and "Impressionist" Criticism', *British Journal of Aesthetics*, 17 (1977); 'The Vocabulary of Pater's Criticism and the Psychology of Aesthetics', *British Journal of Aesthetics*, 18 (1978); 'Pater's Criticism: Some Distinctions', *Prose Studies*, 4 (1981); 'Semiotics and Oscar Wilde's Accounts of Art', *British Journal of Aesthetics*, 25 (1985); 'Editing Pater', *English Literature in Transition*, 30 (1987); 'Annotating "Hard" Nineteenth Century Novels', *Essays in Criticism*, 36 (1986); 'Recent Work on Nineteenth Century Prose: "Œuvre", Genre or Discourse?' *Prose Studies*, 10 (1987); 'English in Crisis?', *Essays in Criticism*, 39 (1989). I should like to thank the editors of these journals, T. J. Diffey, Philip Dodd, Robert Langenfeld, and Stephen Wall; and to acknowledge the advice of a former editor of the *British Journal of Aesthetics*, the late Harold Osborne. Some of the ideas about the relationship between Pater, texts, and authority were rehearsed in the introduction to my edition of *Marius the Epicurean* (Oxford, 1986). I would like to acknowledge the help given to me by Josephine Guy, who has acted as an unpaid research assistant, and made many invaluable suggestions. I acknowledge with gratitude my debt to her. I have benefited, too, from the support of my family; from conversations with various colleagues and friends: particularly conversations about Wilde with Russell Jackson; and about Pater with William Shuter, whose ideas about intertextuality in *Plato and Platonism* I first encountered at a conference in Arizona, and which I have found extremely suggestive. I also have older debts to acknowledge: to the late Donald Gordon, the late Ian Fletcher, and the late Richard Ellmann: teachers, examiners, and then friends. I record my debt to my employer, the University of Birmingham, for a sabbatical term in the spring of 1989 which enabled me to put this book into a final form. I am grateful too to the staff of the following institutions: Birmingham University Library, in particular to Ben Benedikz, the Rare Books librarian; to the British Library; and to Birmingham Public Library.

Birmingham 1989   I.S.

Contents

PART I

SCHOLARSHIP AND EPISTEMOLOGY

What we aimed at from a social point of view was a
complete revision of human relations, political, moral and
economic, in the light of science, . . . and an unsparing
reform of whatever, in the judgement of science.

Henry Sidgwick, *A Memoir*.

1

Introduction

The years between 1865 and 1890 saw a flowering of critical writing in Britain. Indeed, it is possible to see those years as a time peculiarly devoted to the writing of criticism and to writing about criticism, so much so that it is the non-fictional prose of the period, rather than the prose fictions, drama, or poetry, which is now remembered. Some of the major figures are so famous that they scarcely need to be listed—they include John Ruskin, Matthew Arnold, Walter Pater, James McNeill Whistler, William Morris, and Oscar Wilde: all devoted considerable time and energy to writing criticism and to theorizing about it. Moreover, during those twenty-five years the nature of critical writing itself underwent profound changes.

This work is an attempt to explain and analyse those changes in the theory and practice of critical writing. It has grown out of a conviction that recent histories of the literature and criticism of the period are inadequate simply because they have asked inappropriate questions. An ambition to write a prolegomenon to a history of criticism may strike the reader as a curiously modest one: in fact it is more ambitious than it at first seems to be. My overarching concern is to characterize the nature of institutional and intellectual authority in critical discourse in the final decades of the nineteenth century; and in so doing I shall examine the sociology of knowledge in Britain from the 1870s to the 1890s. Finally I suggest that such a methodology might possess a general applicability, particularly for understanding the practice of literary criticism at the present time.

Recently literary historians writing about the last decades of the nineteenth century have tended to tax writers with questions that they simply could not have known about, or would not have considered relevant *had* they known about them. In this respect, recent projects in literary criticism which have

AN ÆSTHETIC MIDDAY MEAL.

*At the Luncheon hour, Jellaby Postlethwaite enters a Pastrycook's and calls for a glass of Water,
into which he puts a freshly-cut Lily, and loses himself in contemplation thereof.*

Waiter. "SHALL I BRING YOU ANYTHING ELSE, SIR?"
Jellaby Postlethwaite. "THANKS, NO! I HAVE ALL I REQUIRE, AND SHALL SOON HAVE DONE!"

George Du Maurier, 'An Aesthetic Midday Meal', *Punch*, 79
(17 July 1880), 23

attempted to 'reread' or 'rewrite' aspects of literary history in order to find issues important for contemporary feminist or Marxist or structuralist thinking are nothing more than forms of latter-day intellectual *midrash*: they ask questions about the past which almost certainly would have been irrelevant *then*, and thus, under the rubric of some general political concern, simply falsify the past. The result is not just bad *intellectual* history, although it is clearly that, but bad *history* also, for such an approach says nothing about the *historical* conditions which produced a certain discourse at a certain moment in time. I propose that in studying the history of criticism, we should address the wider intellectual context of the past, because it was these issues which were instrumental in determining the forms which criticism took. In the last decades of the nineteenth century, the most important of these issues were those which decided the nature of intellectual authority, particularly the relationship between authority and epistemology in various disciplines of thought.

From this modest beginning, then, a much stronger and more comprehensive argument can be made. Critical practice is so deeply embedded in cultural and intellectual assumptions that a knowledge of the relationship between it and those assumptions is a pre-condition for understanding it. Moreover, if this project to locate literary and critical discourse within a contemporary sociology of knowledge has any value, then its methods will also be applicable to other times, particularly to modern debates about the nature of critical theories. That, however, is a separate study.

In order to give substance to my claims about the transformation in the nature of art and literary criticism in the last century, it will be useful initially to provide some examples by way of a context and an illustration. In 1880 *Punch* published one of George Du Maurier's most barbed lampoons of the Aesthetic Movement. It was a cartoon depicting a languid, long-haired, and quite clearly entranced young man (Jellaby Postlethwaite, an Aesthete who frequently occurred in Du Maurier's work) mooning over a flower placed in the centre of a table in a pastry-cook's shop or cafe. (See Figure.) Underneath the cartoon, which was entitled *An Aesthetic Midday Meal*, was Du Maurier's caption:

At the Luncheon hour, Jellaby Postlethwaite enters a Pastrycook's and calls for a glass of Water, into which he puts a freshly-cut Lily, and loses himself in contemplation thereof.

Waiter. 'Shall I bring you anything else, Sir?'
Jellaby Postlethwaite. 'Thanks, no! I have all I require, and shall soon have done!'[1]

At the level of simple social reference, the cartoon's target was fairly clear. It was the extravagant cult of beauty popularly associated with the names of Oscar Wilde and James McNeill Whistler, and in particular the exaggerated praise bestowed on an assorted and apparently quite random set of objects prized by Aesthetes for their alleged formal qualities and 'aesthetic perfection'—objects such as blue china, peacocks' feathers, lilies, sunflowers, and so on. It is worth noting in passing that the heterogeneity of that group, containing as it does three naturally occurring objects and only one artefact, should have alerted literary historians more than it has done. However the iconographic reference of Du Maurier's work operates at a deeper, more embedded level than this. What is of interest in the cartoon is not just the attitude of Jellaby Postlethwaite to his lily, but the attitude of the unnamed pastry-shop waiter to Postlethwaite himself. He, like scores of 'lesser' mortals in Du Maurier's work, is simply unaware of the extravagant beauty of the flower; so much so that Postlethwaite's obsessive and excessive contemplation of it, instead of eating lunch, is simply absurd. The reason that Postlethwaite is so enchanted by the lily is that he is different from ordinary mortality, particularly waiters. He is allegedly 'gifted' with a set of perceptual faculties that are not the possession of lesser men and women. In popular lampoons or parodies of the Aesthetic Movement, such as Du Maurier's cartoons, or Gilbert and Sullivan's comic opera *Patience*, it is made emphatically clear that those faculties can be engaged by a wide variety of naturally occurring *or* man-made objects; but it is the operation of those faculties which constitutes the resulting experience as an experience of beauty. (Again it ought to be noted in passing, that for social observers such as Du Maurier, claims of this sort were clearly ludicrous: the point of many of his cartoons is that characters such as

---

[1] George Du Maurier, 'An Aesthetic Midday Meal', *Punch*, 79 (17 July 1880), 23.

Postlethwaite are invariably feigning, and can only register their experiences by a series of meaningless exclamations such as 'How utter!' or 'How consummate!') Within the programmes for Aestheticism, principally in those extravagant claims for the autonomy of the sensibility made by such propagandists as Wilde and Whistler, it is the 'attitude' of the Aesthete which creates the conditions for his experiences to be experiences of beauty; and it is the *capacity* for this 'attitude' which differentiates the Postlethwaites or the Maudles (another favourite name for the Aesthete in Du Maurier's cartoons) from 'ordinary' mortals. Obviously Du Maurier's work captured something central to high artistic culture in Britain in the 1880s—it is impossible to explain his popularity as a satirist in any other way; and certainly his cartoons re-enact at a parodic level the injections of Wilde, Whistler, or Pater, or many other lesser lights of the Aesthetic Movement. For the serious apologist for Aestheticism, the experience of beauty did not simply *contrast* with the prosaic experiences or realities of ordinary life: it was an experience of a quite different order. Experience of the 'real' world (the world of the waiter and other customers in the pastry-cook's shop, for example) was, as it were, suspended or superseded by the more vivid, and perceptually distinct, 'world' of art. And such a state of affairs was the consequence of certain perceptual processes: the experience of the world, or anything in it, from an 'aesthetic' point of view, or as the consequence of an 'aesthetic' attitude.

Now there are several simple points to be made about these and similar accounts of art or literature given by the Aesthetes. The first and main point is that it is hard to imagine them occurring earlier in the nineteenth century and virtually impossible to conceive of them occurring in the seventeenth or eighteenth centuries. The reason is fairly obvious: until the middle decades of the nineteenth century it was a commonplace that art was capable of embodying a form of knowledge about the world, and principally a form of moral knowledge. A change began in the late 1860s. Thereafter, art was no longer simply seen as the embodiment of a form of knowledge, and this new view of art was one with profound implications. Although Aestheticism allegedly placed the highest premium on art and literature, in reality it demonstrated how little value both had, considered either as social products or as forms of knowledge. For the Aesthete of the 1870s and 1880s, art and literature, with all the rich social, institutional, political, and moral values which traditionally had been held to be expressed by them, had become reduced to a set of individual aesthetic experiences: and so they had, in nearly all significant respects, become merely private matters. Indeed the whole movement was founded upon the assertion that subjective—rather than inter-subjective, communal, or objective—experiences of art were the only ones which were valuable or indeed possible. As I shall argue in subsequent chapters, behind these arguments and the polemic generated by them, was an attempt to re-instate the value of literature in order to protect its autonomy: to preserve it, as it were, from competing explanations of its value provided by the newly-professionalized literary histor-ians, philologists, and textual scholars. As such, the strategies of the Aesthetes have considerable lessons for contemporary debates about literary theory, for their emphasis upon a concept of the 'literariness' of literature was in stark contrast to the competing professional and institutional explanations then available.

The polemic of the Aesthetic Movement has been seen in other ways, in particular as a simple attempt to resist the orthodoxies of earlier Victorian writers such as John Stuart Mill or Matthew Arnold, and to propagandize the view that both the creation and experience of art should be freed from either social or moral responsibilities.[2] This account is to a certain extent true. So, for example, in his notorious study *William Blake* and his pamphlet *Notes on Essays and Reviews*, Algernon Swinburne had denied that the writer of a work of literature had any responsibility to ensure that his work was morally educative.[3] But in fact what was also at issue was not simply the *function* of art, but rather its *nature*. A position similar to that which can be deduced from Du Maurier's cartoons had been formally stated by Walter Pater in *Studies in the History of the*

[2] See e.g. R. V. Johnson, *Aestheticism* (London, 1969); or William Gaunt, *The Aesthetic Adventure* (1945; revd. edn., London, 1975); or Graham Hough, *The Last Romantics* (London, 1949).

[3] See Algernon Charles Swinburne, *William Blake* (London, 1868); id., *Notes on Poems and Reviews* (London, 1866).

Renaissance in 1873.[4] Pater's first declaration was that the real value of art for the spectator or reader was a much more personal affair than had hitherto been allowed. Hence the main issue which Pater addresses is that of pleasure:

The objects with which aesthetic criticism deals—music, poetry, artistic and accomplished forms of human life—are indeed recept-acles of so many powers or forces: they possess, like natural elements, so many virtues or qualities. What is this song or picture, this engaging personality presented in life or in a book, to *me*? What effect does it really produce on me? . . . The aesthetic critic, then, regards all the objects with which he has to do, all works of art, and the fairer forms of nature and human life, as powers or forces producing pleasurable sensations each of a more or less peculiar and unique kind.[5]

The point to notice here is that, in Pater's view, what consti-tutes the most significant feature of any aesthetic response is the *relationship* which exists between the spectator or the reader and the artefact or art-object. But it is abundantly clear from Pater's professed concern with the 'fairer forms of nature and human life' (and from Postlethwaite's enraptured flower-gazing), that the aesthetic experience envisaged by the Aesthetes was of a sort which did not *necessarily* involve the presence of art or artefacts. Art was in general sense important for it, but it was certainly not a necessary pre-condition. It was, as we have seen from Du Maurier's cartoon, an attitude which could engage any naturally occurring phenomenon or object, and if the principal concern of the Aesthetic critic was solely an affective state in the mind of the perceiver, then this was a perfectly admissible and logical position to take. Pater, once more in the preface to *The Renaissance*, ran together the following *categories* of objects: 'the picture, the landscape, the engaging personality in life or in a book, *La Gioconda*, the hills of Carrara, Pico of Mirandula': naturally occurring objects or scenes; persons living or dead or fictional; representations: all these were the

---

[4] Walter H. Pater, *Studies in the History of the Renaissance* (London, 1873). Pater's book was substantially revised twice during his lifetime. In the text I shall refer to the most easily available, and best, scholarly edition, that edited by Donald Hill (Berkeley and Los Angeles, 1980), which prints the 1893 text; but unless I note otherwise, I shall quote the form of the 1873 text.

[5] Ibid., xix–xx.

legitimate objects of study for Pater's ideal critic.[6] Victorian writing on art up to the mid-1860s had taken as its subject either works of art or artefacts and the social and moral circumstances which accorded to them their status as 'art'. Hence the first point which arises from this observation is that the kind of critical writing instigated or given prominence by Pater and Swinburne, and the writing produced by the tradition against which they were reacting, did not necessarily agree upon what they could legitimately discuss. One limited its concern to 'aesthetic states' or attitudes (and, in so doing, to psychological affects) and the other to art-objects, their origin, and what they expressed. This qualification leads to a second and more profound point. One of the most significant issues in the numerous critical controversies in the late nineteenth century was that theories of art were confronting, perhaps for the first time in the history of British culture, theories of aesthetic experience, and each particular theory marked out for itself a different area of applicability.

What had happened to produce such a state of affairs? Why was there such a chasm between the modest ambitions which Pater had for art, including, as they did, the apparent relegation of the experience of art to the level of only one—albeit the most reliable—of a number of experiences of pleasure, and those much grander claims about the centrality of art for a society which had been so consistently made earlier in the century? My intention in this work is to explain *why* such a position came about. But first the nature and scope of the change. It can best be seen by placing Pater's arguments and Du Maurier's cartoons against some representative texts from earlier in the century. Perhaps the most useful yardstick against which to measure changes in critical attitudes is a discussion of poetry made by John Stuart Mill in 1833. In that year Mill contributed to the *Monthly Repository* two short essays on poetry which were later reprinted together as 'Thoughts on Poetry and Its Varieties'.[7] The later title is revealing, for Mill claims that

---

[6] Pater, *Studies in the History of the Renaissance*, xx.

[7] John Stuart Mill, 'What is Poetry?' *Monthly Repository*, NS 7 (Jan. 1833), 60–70; id., 'Two Kinds of Poetry', *Monthly Repository*, NS 7 (Oct. 1833), 714–24. Both essays were originally published pseudonymously. See id., 'Some Thoughts on Poetry and Its Varieties', in *Collected Works of John Stuart Mill, Autobiography and Literary Essays*, ed. John M. Robson and Jack Stillinger (London, 1981), 343–65.

poetry cannot be defined in terms of its formal features or attributes. 'Poetry' can inhere within any discourse, for it is a form of 'truth' and consequently independent of considerations such as style, or genre, or structural and formal distinctions in general. Mill is clearly asserting that the pre-condition for all art is that it is capable of embodying a form of knowledge, and it is precisely this attribute which constitutes its 'poetic' qualities. Mill later writes of the culturally common, and hence widely available, symbolic knowledge and values which art embodies and expresses. That this knowledge is articulated through a particular work is sufficient ground for that work to be designated as art or literature: what expresses or embodies this shared symbolic knowledge *is axiomatically art or literature*.[8] The formal qualities of an artefact, such as the stylistic features of a work of literature, are secondary matters in the sense that they may indeed be necessary qualities but, taken alone, they are not sufficient for a work to be designated as art or literature. Mill's case illustrates perfectly the concepts of art and of audience which the aestheticism of Pater was to be so instrumental in challenging.

Mill's methods of argument are, in one way, the demonstration of his case. He begins by appealing not to any logical argument, but to common usage of the term 'poetry'. It is this usage, the common cultural knowledge alluded to in the general currency of the term, which he cites as his first evidence. Nowhere in nineteenth-century criticism is the common social, cultural (and hence, in its widest sense, symbolic) value of art more succinctly described:

The distinction between poetry and what is not poetry, whether explained or not, is felt to be fundamental: and where every one feels a difference, a difference there must be.[9]

Mill goes on to argue that poetry embodies what every 'sane-minded reader' would assent to: that it asserts a continuity of shared value:

---

[8] An account of the symbolic nature of poetry, similar in some respects to that made by Mill, has been argued by Dan Sperber, *Rethinking Symbolism*, tr. Alice L. Morton (Cambridge, 1975).

[9] Mill, 'Some Thoughts on Poetry', 343.

[P]oetry, which is the delineation of the deeper and more secret workings of human emotion, is interesting only to those whom it recalls what they have felt, or whose imagination it stirs up to conceive what they could feel, or what they might have been able to feel had their outward circumstances been different.

Poetry, when it is really such, is truth; and fiction also, if it is good for anything, is truth: but they are different truths. The truth of poetry is to paint the human soul truly: the truth of fiction is to give a true picture of life.[10]

One of the significant points to be made about this argument is that some of the distinctions which a modern literary critic or philosopher of art might want to make—about the fictionality and artefactuality of fiction, or about the possible interrelationships of the mimetic and expressive concepts of art which Mill invokes—are either considered to be unimportant or simply ignored. Mill *appears* to be making a distinction between the mimetic qualities of fiction and the expressive functions of poetry; but the distinction is not sustained. For Mill's purposes, imitative art (here prose fiction) is reproductive of things, and expressive art (here poetry) is reproductive of inner states and feelings. In Mill's view, both the mimetic and expressive aspects of art or literature testify in similar ways to a community of shared perception and feeling existing in both author and audience. Taken to its logical conclusion, of course, such an account of art or literature has no place for the critic, who is simply unnecessary. Mill was, however, a little more cautious than this, for he did in fact envisage a set of explanatory tasks for the critic: it was the function of criticism to render more easily and more widely available the symbolic knowledge which poetry or art embodies. The critic, then, articulated for less capable minds what must axiomatically be present in any 'poetic' utterance.

These ideas were more fully set out in a letter to Thomas Carlyle in which Mill commented upon the two pieces which he had written for the *Monthly Repository*. He saw Carlyle's gifts as essentially those of the poet and his own as essentially those of the critic. The piece is worth quoting at length for a number of reasons. In the first place it is a central account of the idea that

---

[10] Mill, 'Some Thoughts on Poetry', 345–6.

both the critic and the poet are engaged in expounding a set of symbolic (or 'intuitive') truths. More importantly, however, it demonstrates how necessary Mill considered art, literature, and criticism to be to a culture; and, by extension, it shows how marginal, in cultural terms, art and literature had become by the time Du Maurier was drawing his cartoons for *Punch*. In his letter Mill distinguished between two sorts of knowledge, the symbolic and the logical, which pertained to intuitive and empirical experience respectively. The function of the critic was to render one form of knowledge amenable to description in terms of the other:

I conceive that most of the highest truths are, to persons endowed by nature in certain ways which I think I could state, intuitive; that is, they need neither explanation nor proof, but if not known before, are assented to as soon as stated. Now it appears to me that the poet or artist is conversant chiefly with *such* truths and that his office in respect to truth is to declare *them*, and to make them *impressive*. This, however, supposes that the reader, hearer, or spectator is a person of the kind to whom those truths *are* intuitive. Such will of course receive them at once, and will lay them to heart in proportion to the impressiveness with which the artist delivers and embodies them. But the other and more numerous kind of people will consider them as nothing but dreaming or madness: and the more so, certainly, the more powerful the artist, *as* an artist: because the means which are good for rendering the truth impressive to those who know it, are not the same and are often absolutely incompatible with those which render it intelligible to those who know it not. Now this last I think is the proper office of the logician or I might say the metaphysician, in truth he must be both. The same person may be poet and logician, but he cannot be both in the same composition.

Mill then goes on to define the relationship between the functions of the poet and of the critic in terms of knowledge:

The artist's is the highest part, for by him alone is real *knowledge* of such truths conveyed: but it is possible to convince him who never could *know* the intuitive truths, that they are not inconsistent with anything he *does* know; that they are even very *probable*, and that he may have faith in them when higher natures than his own affirm that they are truths. He may then build on them and act on them, or at least act nothing contradictory to them. Now this humbler part is, I think, that which is most suitable to my faculties, as a man of speculation. I am not in the least a poet, in any sense; but I can do homage to poetry. I can to a very considerable extent feel it and understand it, and can make others who are my inferiors understand it in proportion to the measure of their capacity. I believe that such a person is more wanted than even the poet himself; that there are more persons living who approximate to the latter character than to the former. . . . Now one thing not useless to do would be to exemplify this difference by enlarging in my logical fashion upon the difference itself: to make those who are not poets, understand that poetry is higher than Logic, and that the union of the two is Philosophy.[11]

The final yoking of poetry, logic, and philosophy is of course a Romantic commonplace, but it is none the less an instructive one, for in Mill's eyes, poetry is an enterprise the cultural worth of which is fixed. The poet's function in society, the possibilities for successful creative work, and its subsequent appropriation by that society—all these in Mill's view were determined by a general concept of art. That concept inevitably involved ethics and metaphysics; moreover, the aesthetic described here by Mill was fundamentally expressive in character, in the sense that in his view the poet first expressed or exteriorized internal feelings, and secondly facilitated the exteriorization of similar feelings in the reader. What was distinctly 'poetic' in all art was not a set of formal attributes or features, nor the product of a series of attitudes brought to it by the reader or spectator, but rather its capacity to embody certain forms of moral and symbolic knowledge.

The arguments of Du Maurier, Pater, and Mill show dramatic moments in a process of change in artistic and literary culture. Certainties about the role of criticism and its relation to art and literature disappeared in the years between Mill's letter and Pater's essay, so much so that critics after 1870 had no simple and stable concept of literary or pictorial art to draw upon, and could make no simple appeal to a universally acknowledged standard of authority to underwrite their critical judgements. The extent of this change is evidenced by the fact that critics writing in the years between Mill's letter and Pater's essay felt the need to argue the case for the cultural significance of poetry, rather than merely to assert it in the manner in which

[11] John Stuart Mill, letter to Thomas Carlyle (5 July 1833), in *Collected Works of John Stuart Mill*, xii. *Earlier Letters of John Stuart Mill 1812–1848*, ed. Francis E. Mineka (London, 1963), 162–3.

Mill had done. Nor, after about 1860, could any critic take as axiomatic the proposition that criticism was instrumental in propounding the 'intuitive' truths of poetry—certainly not with the confidence which Mill had shown. The relevance of criticism to a national culture, too, was a case that had to be argued, most elaborately, perhaps by Matthew Arnold in *Culture and Anarchy* and 'The Function of Criticism at the Present Time' in *Essays in Criticism* in the mid- and late 1860s.[12] Indeed, one of Arnold's constant preoccupations was to promote an intellectual culture as a means of achieving social and political stability. 'The Function of Criticism' argues for the centrality of criticism in creating an environment in which such an intellectual culture might occur. In fact Arnold's career coincided with the increasing impracticality of such an ambition. The unashamed subjectivism of Du Maurier's Aesthetes represents a further point in the process of the marginalization of art, literature, and criticism in terms of their inability any longer to embody and to articulate symbolic and moral value.

How are these changes in intellectual history to be explained? Here we immediately encounter two distinct sets of problems, the first concerning types of history and the second concerning definitions of what specific intellectual practices are to count as intellectual history. The most usual first step in documenting the history of criticism in the final years of the nineteenth century is to define what is to count as criticism. But this definition frequently refers to the work of a rather narrow set of authors who are invariably chosen for their current, and not their contemporary, prestige.[13] They are then ranged into a history, the purpose of which is to explain the origins and significance of *modern* critical debates. Such an odd historiographical tactic makes many unjustified assumptions, the most important of which is that it takes what it seeks in the first place to explain—a history of criticism—as a given of history. Thus typically, within the period with which I am concerned, a history of criticism from, say, Ruskin and Arnold to Eliot and

---

[12] See Matthew Arnold, *Culture and Anarchy* (London, 1869); id., 'The Function of Criticism at the Present Time', *Essays in Criticism* (London, 1865).

[13] These histories are too numerous to list in any detail, but they include the work of historians as diverse as René Wellek, *History Of Modern Criticism*, iv (London, 1965), and Raymond Williams, *Culture and Society 1780–1950* (London, 1958).

Leavis, is described within terms of tradition and continuity: it is usually argued that these critics are broadly concerned with the same issues and so address them in broadly the same manner.[14] (Whether these critics are then seen to be successful or not naturally depends in its turn upon the prejudices of the historian in question.) Critics whose work consorts oddly with that tradition—Pater, Whistler, and Wilde, for example—or critics whose work is now deemed to be historically insignificant—such as Walter Besant—are customarily and cursorily explained in terms of aberrance or heterodoxy.

In *Philosophy in History* the American philosopher Richard Rorty identifies four distinct genres in the history of thought. His last genre, which he calls 'doxography', he characterizes by its attempts to tell a story of intellectual progress by describing canonical texts in terms of contemporary or recent intellectual orthodoxies. Such 'doxographies', in Rorty's view, are of little use for they simply misrepresent intellectual history:

[D]oxography is the attempt to impose a problematic on a canon drawn up without reference to that problematic, or, conversely, to impose a canon on a problematic constructed without reference to that canon. . . . [T]he real trouble with doxography is that it is a *half-hearted* attempt to tell a new story of intellectual progress by describing all texts in the light of recent discoveries.[15]

It might be objected that Rorty's categories are too severely defined, or that his programme for an intellectual history is too ambitious,[16] but none the less it is in a category broadly similar to doxography that I would wish to place many recent histories of nineteenth-century criticism. Most of these histories perceive the value of all critical enterprises from the privileged vantage-

---

[14] See e.g. Chris Baldick, *The Social Mission of English Criticism 1848–1932* (Oxford, 1983).

[15] Richard Rorty, 'Historiography of Philosophy: Four Genres', in Richard Rorty, J. B. Schneewind and Quentin Skinner (eds.), *Philosophy in History* (Cambridge, 1984), 62–3.

[16] Ideas of historical context and of value have recently been discussed in relation to debates about the merit of historicism in literary history. In particular the 'New' historicism of cultural materialists has been contrasted with the uses of historical research by literary historians. (See e.g. Howard Felperin, 'Making it "Neo": The New Historicism and Renaissance Literature', *Textual Practice*, 1 (1987), 262–77.) But such arguments are concerned principally with the use of history in explaining literary artefacts, and as such seem of limited applicability to intellectual history.

point of the present, and consequently the relationship of critical writing of the past to present concerns is taken to be the main, and sometimes the only, point of interest. One of the alternatives posed by Rorty to this 'false' history is the genre he calls 'Geistesgeschichten': a history of ideas which attempts to discover why certain questions became central to certain disciplines of thought at certain moments in the past:

[W]e need more and better contextualist historical reconstructions on the one hand, and more self-confident *Geistesgeschichte* on the other. We need to realize that the questions which the 'contingent arrangements' of the present time lead us to regard as *the* questions are questions which may be *better* than those which our ancestors asked, but need not be the *same*. They are not questions which any reflective human being must necessarily have encountered. . . . It is one thing to say that a great dead philosopher would have been driven to have a view on a certain topic if we had had a chance to talk to him, thus enabling him to see what the fundamental questions of philosophy really were. It is another thing to say that he had an 'implicit' view on that topic which we can dig out of what he wrote. What is interesting about him often is that it never crossed his mind that he had to have a view on the topic. This is just the sort of interesting information we get from contextualist historical reconstructions.[17]

The present work attempts to be this kind of intellectual history.

None the less there still remains the more prosaic problem of how to choose which specific practices count as evidence in a history of critical thought. Here, once more, recent histories of criticism have avoided rather than elucidated the issues, principally because they have almost universally tended to assume that there is a simple set of practices and a simple discipline of knowledge which may be characterized as 'criticism'. Such a claim is far from being self-evidently true, at least in the manner in which its apologists have blithely assumed. Indeed the truth of the opposite case is much more likely. Here the real question is, What precisely are the social and intellectual practices which the terms 'literary criticism' and 'art criticism' have been used to define? Some deliberately incongruous examples will make my point clear. For an historian to

[17] Rorty, 'Historiography of Philosophy', 63–4.

describe the work of, say, John Ruskin and Roland Barthes as criticism is to presuppose that their work can be meaningfully compared; to presuppose, that is, historical and geographical circumstances aside, that they are doing the same 'thing'. But the general movements in intellectual history suggest that indeed they might not be doing the same 'thing' in so far as the assumptions upon which their criticism is posited differ so enormously and so obviously. Ruskin and Barthes invoke vastly different anthropologies and epistemologies to validate both their objects of study and their intellectual practices. In Barthes's case, structuralism has found in the literary text an expression of common *langue* rather than individual (that is authorial) *parole*, and so, for example, post-Saussurean structuralist criticism depends in the first place upon a linguistic model of human activity, upon the concept of man as a sign-making animal, to validate it. Ruskin's early criticism depends in its turn upon a specifically religious epistemology, especially as it relates to the concept of 'types', to define what is to be considered representatively 'beautiful'. Concepts of meaning, therefore, in the works of both writers, whatever local agreements or disagreements there might be, are derived from quite different origins.

Two further examples will make my general point clearer. Ernest Jones's famous essay on *Hamlet* rests upon prior assumptions about the relationship between creativity and human mental operations as they are described by psychoanalysis: namely, that literary artefacts stand in an expressive relationship to their authors, that this expressive relationship is psychologically determined and determinative, and that the methodology of psychoanalysis can reveal the real nature of that relationship. Without these assumptions, Jones's comments on *Hamlet* simply have no logic. (This is not to say that they are right, simply that they are consistent with the premisses of psychoanalysis.) Or, to take an example more familiar perhaps to the modern reader: Marxist criticism depends upon what Michel Foucault has called an 'economic' model of human activity to validate its practices and observations. If readers fail to agree with this basic assumption of Marxist theory, then Marxist literary criticism can have no relevance nor coherence for them.

What each of these examples demonstrates is that the terms 'literary' or 'art' criticism do not describe a well-defined body of knowledge and set of practices. Historically criticism has derived its principles of validation and its intellectual authority, its methods of enquiry and its modes of operation, from other —and often quite separate and usually more systematic— disciplines of knowledge. And it has done so covertly, almost illicitly, in so far as the nature of its theoretical dependence and its intellectual debts are rarely apparent from its practices.

The epistemological and anthropological assumptions which underlie the criticism of the past have not been acknowledged, let alone adequately described. Absent from most histories of criticism is a recognition that one particular aspect of past cultures needs to be recovered—the intellectual structures of past disciplines of knowledge and their relations to each other. Paradoxically, it is the criticism of the more distant past which has been best served in this respect;[18] the criticism of the late nineteenth century has to a large extent been neglected in the senses outlined above. It has of course been well documented—as, for example, a discourse which relates in a general manner to British social history, or, as I have indicated, as a discourse which is autonomous and allegedly obeys rules of its own logic. But all such histories seem in their turn to assume that both the nature of criticism, and, more importantly, decisions about *what has counted as good criticism*, are simple and unproblematic.

My project is thus a simple one. It derives from the observation that such debates about criticism were a part of, and were indeed partly caused by, much larger upheavals in British intellectual life. These upheavals were felt in three ways. First, as I shall describe in later chapters, in changes in the models of 'man', which in many disciplines of knowledge, particularly those in the newly emergent social sciences, were used to underwrite the explanations of their practices. Secondly, they were felt in the crisis of intellectual authority which affected all disciplines of knowledge and which thus profoundly altered the

---

[18] See e.g. the work of Paul Oskar Kristeller on the history of the concept of art in 'Modern System of the Arts: A Study in the History of Aesthetics: (I)', *Journal of the History of Ideas*, 12 (1951), 496–527, and id., 'Modern System of the Arts: A Study in the History of Aesthetics: (II)', *Journal of the History of Ideas*, 13 (1952), 17–46.

value of particular critical statements. The third main change which affected the nature of literary criticism in the years between Mill's letter to Carlyle and Du Maurier's lampoons of Aestheticism was the fact that, along with many other disciplines, criticism became institutionalized within the universities: indeed, as I shall show, one of the main ends of university reform in the last half of the nineteenth century was to accommodate the growing diversity of intellectual enquiry. More importantly, along with the process of institutionalization went the companion process of professionalization. Taken together, institutionalization and professionalization had profound effects upon the authorization of all kinds of knowledge, including literary criticism, and these effects are still being felt today.

This process of professionalization needs to be described, but what follows is a brief and a necessarily very partial account of it. My summary is intended to stress only those aspects of professionalization which are relevant to the main subject-matter of this book—the relationship between authority and knowledge. The general process of professionalization which took place in the second half of the nineteenth century is important in so far as it affected the ways in which knowledge was organized and authorized. All intellectuals and academics, willingly or unwillingly, had to come to terms with these changes and, as we shall see, they did so in very different ways: at one extreme of the range of reactions was the wholesale rejection of professional values by writers such as Pater and Wilde; while at the other was the almost Messianic embrace of them by aspiring professional academic critics such as John Churton Collins; and in between was the reluctant but resigned acceptance which characterized then (and still does now) many university dons' attitudes to any reform.

In Britain, it is generally recognized that the professions as we know them today were a Victorian product, brought into being to serve the needs of an increasingly complex industrial society. The first census to include the professions was conducted in 1841, and by the end of the century the three ancient professions—law, divinity, and physic[19]—had been joined by

---

[19] The name 'physic' refers to non-surgical medicine. The professionalization of surgery took place at a considerably later date. The professional distinction between physicians and surgeons of course continues to the present day.

most of those we recognize today—accountancy, dentistry, engineering, surveying, and so forth. With the growth of science and technology throughout the whole of the nineteenth century, knowledge tended to become more abundant, more complex, and thus more specialized; to be competent required an individual to concentrate upon one particular field of enquiry, and to undertake an increasingly specialized training. One of the results of this change was a process which has been labelled the 'rise of the expert'. A consequence of this rise was the undermining of the authority of the Victorian 'sage': the eminence of the 'man of letters' gradually gave way to the greater specialist knowledge of the professional. The history of this process has been documented elsewhere and its specific details are not relevant here.[20] However, what is of interest is the manner in which the ideas associated with the general process of professionalization and specialization impinged upon the universities, and thus upon intellectuals and academics. In particular, the process of professionalization exercised an influence upon the pattern of university reform. Indeed it can be argued that those reforms in themselves were an attempt to give universities a more professional status, a strategy which was an inevitable response to the growing demand and respect for specialist knowledge. To maintain their prestige, universities, in a way not dissimilar from today, had to adapt themselves to compete with the newly professionalized world. The relationship between the universities and the professions has always been very close: professions need universities, but in their turn universities are affected by the idea of professionalization and the criteria (of competence, accountability, relevance, and so forth) which the professions were instrumental in establishing. As Bernard Barber has suggested, the university performs a vital function for the professions, in that it trains future practitioners within a particular profession and formally tests their competence through examinations; and by continual modernization and improvement of knowledge through research, the university ensures the maintenance of standards on behalf of the profession in question. The consequence of this

[20] See W. J. Reader, *Professional Men: The Rise of the Professional Classes in Nineteenth-Century England* (London, 1966).

exchange is that the profession retains its status within a society. Hence nearly every well-established profession is located in some form or other within the university structure, and nearly all nascent or aspiring professions seek to locate themselves within that structure.[21] (It should be remembered that in the nineteenth century the term 'universities' effectively referred to Oxford and Cambridge, and that this situation changed only slowly with the establishment of the civic universities in the last three decades of the century. It is worth noting also that, generally speaking, Cambridge was much more ready to adapt itself than Oxford was.[22]) In the last quarter of the nineteenth century, the university syllabus expanded to include subjects such as history and English.[23] This change was largely in response to continual pressure from both individuals and from various interest groups who wished to see their particular practices authorized. By the last two decades of the nineteenth century, to give authority to a particular practice or body of knowledge required the professional status which only the university, or some similar institution, could bestow. Thus there were two ways in which the process of professionalization in the nineteenth century affected the universities: first, there was the attempt to accommodate the needs of the newly emerging professions by establishing new subjects within the universities; and second, there was the attempt to reorganize the practices of the universities themselves along more professional lines, a process which can be seen both in general university reforms, and in particular reforms in different disciplines.

There is a great deal of sociological literature devoted to the

---

[21] Bernard Barber, 'Some Problems in the Sociology of Professions', *Daedalus*, 92 (1963), 669–88. It is also true, as Barber has pointed out, that there can be drawbacks in this relationship between the universities and the professions, in what he calls a 'structured strain'. This is due to a conflict of interests between academics' concern with 'increasing knowledge and higher moral standards' and the pressures imposed on the profession by 'other cultural and social interests', a conflict all too obvious in present-day universities.

[22] For the differences between the attitudes of Oxford and Cambridge towards reform, see Philippa Levine, *The Amateur and the Professional: Antiquarians, Historians and Archaeologists in Victorian England 1838–1886* (Cambridge, 1986).

[23] For the way in which professionalization affected popular disciplines such as history, see A. T. Milne, 'History and the Universities: Then and Now', *History*, 59 (1974), 33–46.

professions—it is in itself a 'specialism' within sociology—and also a great deal of disagreement over how those professions should be defined.[24] Broadly speaking sociology tends to characterize the professions in terms of 'structures' and 'functions' (although there is also a school of thought which analyses professions in terms of 'traits'). There are several general problems in each of these approaches: notoriously the first two are accused of being ahistorical, and hence unable to account for contradictions and changes within professions, and of being naïvely reliant upon the professionals' own rationalization or assessment of their status. The 'traits' school in its turn always has problems with comprehensiveness—it has to generate endless 'subcategories' needed to account for both the many subtle cultural and historical differences between professions and for the contradictions within them. Moreover, literary historians who are interested in the structures of universities and who deploy sociological analyses have had special problems in using such categories.[25] Nevertheless sociology can offer a rough framework for discussion.[26] Bernard Barber has argued that professionalization is 'always a matter of degree'; and although his argument, based as it is on twentieth-century American examples, has only an approximate relevance to different cultures and different times, it none the less provides a useful point of departure. Barber lists four major attributes of professions. These are:

[A] high degree of generalized and systematic knowledge; primary orientation to the community interest rather than to individual

---

[24] See e.g. the edition of *Daedalus*, 92 (1963) devoted to the professions; A. H. Halsey and M. A. Trow, *The British Academics* (London, 1971); J. A. Jackson (ed.), *Professions and Professionalization* (Cambridge, 1970); M. S. Larson, *The Rise of Professionalism: A Sociological Analysis* (London, 1970); G. Millerson, *Qualifying Associations: A Study in Professionalization* (London, 1964); Talcot Parsons, 'Professions' in D. L. Sills (ed.), *International Encyclopaedia of the Social Sciences*, xii (1968), 536–47; W. J. Reader, *Professional Men*; Émile Durkheim, *Professional Ethics and Civil Morals*, tr. Cornelia Brookfield (London, 1957); William J. Goode, 'Community within a Community: The Professions', *American Sociological Review*, 22 (1957), 194–200; Philip Elliot, *Sociology of the Professions* (London, 1972); Andrew Abbott, 'Status and Strain in the Professions', *American Journal of Sociology*, 86 (1981), 819–35.

[25] See Doris Goldstein, 'The Professionalization of History in the Late Nineteenth and Early Twentieth Centuries', *Storia della storiografia*, 1 (1983), 3–23.

[26] See Robert L. Patten, '"The People have set Literature free": The Professionalization of Letters in Nineteenth-Century England', *Review*, 9 (1987), 1–34.

self-interest; a high degree of self-control of behaviour through codes of ethics internalized in the process of work socialization and through voluntary associations organized and operated by the work specialists themselves; and a system of rewards (monetary and honorary) that is primarily a set of symbols of work achievement and thus ends in themselves, not means to some other end of individual self-interest.[27]

To these we might also add Everett Hughes's emphasis on the 'esoteric' nature of the professions' services, and the professional claim that those services depend upon 'some branch of knowledge to which the professionals are privy by virtue of long study and by initiation and apprenticeship under masters already members of the profession'.[28] Generally speaking, then, the process of professionalization entails laying claim to a specific body of knowledge. That knowledge is valued in so far as it becomes restricted to a specific group of practitioners—to specialists. It is thus no longer the kind of knowledge which the general public may acquire. And the professions then safeguard what is now 'their' knowledge by requiring future practitioners to be specially trained and formally examined. This process assures a certain standard of expertise, essential in retaining public respect, and also maintains the restrictions and exclusions which are necessary for a profession to keep its status and separate identity.

The growth of the professions in Britain along lines such as these coincided with, and was causally related to, the pressure for reform of the universities in Britain. In fact the process of reform occurred over most of the last half of the nineteenth century following the Royal Commission of 1850–2. Specific reforms took place within the university structure—in, for example, pedagogy, entrance qualifications (particularly in the abolition of religious tests), in the introduction of formal written and oral examinations, and in the expansion of the curriculum to include such subjects as natural science, moral science, history, and English, the last being the subject of a lengthy debate in the 1880s, leading finally to the establishment of a school of English in Oxford in 1893. And at different times there were changes to the structure of individual disciplines,

[27] Barber, 'Sociology of Knowledge', 672.
[28] See Everett Hughes, 'Professions', *Daedalus*, 92 (1963), 655–67.

such as history.[29] Underlying these reforms was the general recognition within the universities that they ought to respond to pressure from outside. The expansion of the curriculum to include subjects such as English was also largely the result of 'outside' pressures. As knowledge became more specialized, so various practitioners demanded that their particular area of knowledge be given the status of a separate discipline, and hence be given separate departmental or faculty status within the university structure. Such a state of affairs corresponds very closely to the general pattern of professionalization, for one of the prime claims of professionals is the esoteric nature of their practices; they must, that is, define themselves in opposition or in distinction to other specialisms. The introduction of written examinations within universities was perhaps the most obvious response to the pressures to professionalize. At a time when the status and relevance of universities were in doubt, written examinations (nominally at least) ensured standards were kept, and thus retained the exclusivity which was necessary to safeguard specialist knowledge.

The main point to be made here about the general processes of professionalization and institutionalization which took place in the last half of the nineteenth century is that they permanently affected the ways in which literary criticism was practised and authorized. Indeed, the arguments over the establishment of schools of English in universities in the 1880s made public the inevitability of those changes. Although many interested

---

[29] e.g. William Stubbs's proposals in the early 1870s for reforming historiography in Oxford along the lines suggested by the new German scholarship necessitated wholesale changes in pedagogy, examinations, and so forth. In fact the changes took over twenty years to effect. See Milne, 'History and the Universities'. Other disciplines reformed themselves equally slowly, but at different times. See Doris Goldstein, 'Professionalization of History'. For general discussion of different aspects of university reform, see Sheldon Rothblatt, *Revolution of the Dons* (London, 1968); id., *Tradition and Change in English Liberal Education* (London, 1976); H. B. Charlton, *Portrait of a University 1851–1951* (Manchester, 1951); T. W. Heyck, 'The Idea of a University in Britain 1870–1970' in *History of European Ideas*, 8 (1987), 205–19; id., *Transformation of Intellectual Life in Victorian England* (London, 1982); W. R. Ward, *Victorian Oxford* (London, 1965); Anthony Kearney, *John Churton Collins: The Louse on the Locks of Literature* (Edinburgh, 1985); J. P. C. Roach, 'Victorian Universities and the National Intelligentsia', *Victorian Studies*, 2 (1959), 131–50; Christopher Harvie, *The Lights of Liberalism: University Liberals and the Challenge of Democracy 1860–1886* (London, 1976); John Sparrow, *Mark Pattison and the Idea of a University* (Cambridge, 1967); Melvin Richter, *The Politics of Conscience* (London, 1964).

parties supported the idea that English should enter the curriculum, few were willing to entertain the idea that English could be represented by a separate school within the university. Thus by extension, few allowed that there could ever be a profession of practitioners of English. This issue was at the heart of a long campaign conducted by John Churton Collins, a representative of a 'new' academic type, to whom I shall return. Collins desperately sought to establish the study of vernacular literature in universities and to give to it the authority and prestige which had characterized the study of classical literatures, languages, and cultures. But the model for English studies within universities which Collins proposed was eventually rejected in favour of philology and textual scholarship. Philologists and textual scholars were able to make a much more cogent case for a real specialism—and so for a real profession—because they *did* have access to esoteric knowledge, and, following the German example, did have a specific set of practices which required specific training. None the less the changes brought about by the newly professionalized academic scholars and critics of English permanently marginalized other forms of non-institutional literary criticism.

As later chapters will make clear, these large changes in institutional practices coincided with, and once again were perhaps caused by, equally large-scale changes in virtually all forms of intellectual life in Britain. From around 1860 there was a set of crises in British social science and in related disciplines such as history and psychology. The most significant of these was a crisis in the ideology of political economy which precipitated a series of far-reaching changes in what we now understand as the discipline of economics. Political economy for the latter part of the eighteenth century and first seventy years of the nineteenth was the dominant ideology in Britain, in that it attempted to account for far more than simple economic matters. Rather, it took upon itself explanations of the whole of human behaviour. The criticism by writers such as Thomas Carlyle—in, for example, his outburst in *Past and Present* (1843) that the 'cash-nexus' did not identify the only relationship between human beings[30]—only has significance once the hege-

---

[30] See Thomas Carlyle, *Past and Present*, bk. III, ch. 2 (London, 1843).

mony of political economy is realized. This crisis in the doctrines of classical political economy coincided with a set of
crises in other disciplines of knowledge, particularly in historiography, sociology, and psychology. In these senses, then,
political economy can serve as a paradigm to examine the
relationship between intellectual authority and epistemology
in mid-century Victorian intellectual life.

A consequence of these crises was a transformation in the
status of many disciplines of knowledge. Once more, the history
of political economy is paradigmatic. Despite criticisms, such
as those of Carlyle, or the much more damaging qualification
about the Wages Fund theory in the 1860s by one of its hitherto
most able apologists, John Stuart Mill, political economy was a
dominant, but not a specialized, discipline of knowledge.[31] The
writing of political economy, up to the mid-1870s, was not a
specialist matter. Generally speaking, political economists
were businessmen or politicians: professional or academic
political economists were rare and heavily outnumbered by
their amateur colleagues. After 1870, as classical political
economy lost its authority and thus its dominance, economics,
as a separate discipline of knowledge, emerged; and the practitioners of that discipline *were* specialists. As I have indicated,
this process of specialization and professionalization also took
place in many other disciplines. Moreover, marginalization
was a consequence of specialization in that debates about
economics were henceforward conducted within the confines of
universities (and, even as late as 1900, in a small number of
universities, too). As knowledge became institutionalized and
removed to an academic milieu, so dissent was restricted by
virtue of its being conducted in accordance with the canons of
academic propriety. How competing claims were to be tested,
and what principles were to regulate their intellectual and
institutional acceptance or rejection, these became central
topics. Moreover, the nature of those tests changed, for by
being placed within an academic milieu, intellectual authority
became exclusively textual in nature.

As I have suggested, the consequences of crisis and specialization are particularly easy to see in the case of classical

---

[31] Mill's critique of the Wages Fund theory is discussed in Ch. 2.

political economy. After the 1870s, when political economy had begun to lose its ideological force, it was increasingly in competition with other disciplines of knowledge as a principle of explanation for human affairs. Prior to the 1870s it had provided a *general* explanation of human behaviour; after that decade it had to compete with rival but specialized explanations. Moreover, there were two kinds of intellectual competition at work: the first was a competition between general explanations, such as political economy on the one hand, and individual, specialized explanations on the other. In these senses, what was at issue was a controversy about the nature of *all explanations*: whether they were to be general or specialized. A part of this controversy was a growing sense that if an explanation was scholarly and rigorous, it could as a consequence account for only *part* of human life. The corollary was the insight that the more general, and hence less scholarly and less rigorous, the explanation, the less utility it would prove to possess. There was, however, a second, but equally important, kind of intellectual competition: that occurring between specialisms themselves. Here the issue was how two or more specialized explanations could account for the same set of phenomena. As a consequence of this competition, intellectual authority became the central issue for virtually all disciplines of knowledge in the last decades of the century—in, as I have suggested, economics, history, sociology, psychology, biology, and, as I shall subsequently argue, in literary and art criticism as well. Two large questions follow from these observations. The first is how intellectual authority was invoked, and the second is what validated that authority.

In *The Interpretation of Cultures*, Clifford Geertz discusses the interrelatedness of concepts of culture and concepts of man. He describes the Enlightenment concepts of the irreduceability and universality of human nature—how, in this view, the 'vast variety of differences among men, in beliefs and values, in customs and institutions, both over time and from place to place, is essentially without significance in defining his nature'.[32] Geertz goes on to discuss the decline in the usefulness of this concept in the following terms:

[32] Clifford Geertz, *The Interpretation of Cultures* (London, 1975), 35.

The trouble with this kind of view . . . is that the image of a constant human nature independent of time, place, and circumstance, of studies and professions, transient fashions and temporary opinions, may be an illusion, that what man is may be so entangled with where he is, who he is, and what he believes that it is inseparable from them.[33]

Geertz indicates how, during the course of the nineteenth century, the relationship between concepts of culture and concepts of man came to be seen as a dynamic one: how, that is, the 'cultural' came to be seen as constitutive of the 'human'. Geertz's observations may be extended to account for a salient feature of much nineteenth-century intellectual history. A provisionality about what human nature might be is one of the most significant ways intellectual activity in the nineteenth century can be marked off from that of the eighteenth. Inevitably this unease about the stability of human nature had an effect upon writing about art and literature—particularly about what art and literary criticism was to include in its practices. In passing Geertz mentions Samuel Johnson's famous attempt in the *Preface to Shakespeare* to read on to Shakespeare's characters the anthropological assumptions of the Enlightenment. What is interesting about the history of critical writing in the nineteenth century in this respect is that such assumptions about the typically 'human' are rarely made after about 1830; indeed, after the publication of Darwin's speculations on the relationship of species in the 1850s, concepts such as the universality of human nature are almost never alluded to except in specifically political discourses. What follows from Geertz's general point, then, is that when there is more than one intellectual model of 'man' at any one historical moment—as in the last decades of the nineteenth century—then there will invariably be competition between epistemologies. And if there is competition between epistemologies, the way in which authority is established also becomes problematic. In the late nineteenth century, competing claims about the nature of intellectual authority had as their basis competing models of human nature which were invoked as explanations.

To make my point in general terms: intellectual authority, in

---

[33] Ibid.

the sense that it furnishes coherence in explanations, is always based upon an epistemology. Moreover, when there is a consensus about the appropriateness of this epistemology, intellectual authority is never in dispute; such an observation accounts perfectly for the history of classical political economy in the first half of the nineteenth century. But when that epistemology *is* threatened by competitors—as with the developments in science and social science in the last half of the nineteenth century—then intellectual authority itself becomes problematic. From 1860 onwards, competing epistemologies precipitated a series of crises in the nature of intellectual authority in Britain. These crises had obvious consequences in the disciplines most immediately affected, but they also had implications for less obvious areas of intellectual life.

In a programmatic form, then, the argument underlying this book can be presented very briefly. Authority became the central issue for disciplines of knowledge after 1870, because these disciplines were in competition with each other and offered different explanations of human society. Moreover, the manner in which authority was to be established itself became problematic after 1870 because, as there were competing epistemologies, so there were competing models of authority. This—how the topic of authority was addressed in literary and art criticism—is the real subject of my enquiry.

2

Economics, Historiography, and Sociology

I. POLITICAL ECONOMY

Histories of the development of the social sciences typically place changes in a particular discipline of knowledge into one of two categories: the exogenous and the endogenous. The argument runs along the following lines: in so far as a social science approximates to the methodology of a natural science, changes in its practice and in its theory are produced by an internal dynamic and an internal logic. The general proposition underlying this claim is that the natural sciences, at the level of theoretical speculation, remain immune from influences which originate from outside the discipline in question. However, the social sciences, especially those disciplines concerned not just with theory but also with practice (which in some instances will be social policy), do not enjoy such immunity, and in so far as a social science is affected by institutional and professional factors, changes within it will also be determined exogenously.

This distinction is a useful one, and can be applied to areas of intellectual activity well beyond the social sciences; indeed, as I shall suggest, in some ways it is possible to see changes in critical practices conforming very precisely to it. Thus in literary criticism in the late nineteenth century there were, on the one hand, those sorts of changes which were produced within the practice itself. These included both changes in what was deemed to constitute an appropriate critical statement, and changes in the relationship between criticism and scholarship. And on the other hand, there were the various social, professional, and institutional changes which designated some critical statements as authoritative and others not.[1] The relationship of all this to those changes which were occurring in the social sciences at the same time is not as remote as it might first seem to be. Economics, historiography, sociology, and psychology, all of these disciplines of knowledge underwent profound crises in the decades between 1855 and 1885, crises which determined in what kinds of ways they were to be considered disciplines of knowledge. The changes which occurred in the central British social science, economics, from 1871 onwards may be considered in these respects to be paradigmatic.[2] The theoretical revolution within economics (or to give it its more usual nineteenth-century designation, political economy) exemplifies in a startling way changes endogenous to a discipline of knowledge; but it also illustrates larger movements within the sociology of knowledge in the last three decades of the nineteenth century. Indeed, as Lawrence Birken has argued, it is possible that the changes which occurred in economic thought—its transition from classical political economy in the early years of the century to the emergence of marginal utility theory in the years after 1871—may be seen as epiphenomena produced by 'a much larger cultural shift that took place among transatlantic intellectual circles and across disciplinary lines during the latter part of the nineteenth century'. And Birken has argued also that the 'relativization of value inherent in marginalism' coincided with other forms of relativization in a wide range of intellectual activity.[3] Generally the crisis in many disciplines of knowledge in the 1870s involved changes in their relevant epistemologies; and these epistemological changes in their turn provide a means of exploring the history and sociology of nineteenth-century knowledge.

[1] I do not wish to exclude the possibility that the two might in the end, of course, be related, in the sense that some statements might be deemed to possess authority simply because of features such as internal consistency, scholarly knowledge, and so forth. But these are not the sole grounds for such judgements.

[2] There has been a long debate about the nature of the developments which took place within the history of economics in Britain in the last decades of the nineteenth century. What is not at issue, however, is that radical change *did* occur, with profound changes in how economics—both as a theory and as a discipline of knowledge which affected social policy—was practised: see appendix to Ch. 2.

[3] Lawrence Birken, 'From Macroeconomics to Microeconomics: The Marginalist Revolution in Sociocultural Perspective', *History of Political Economy*, 20 (1988), 252, 260.

The hegemony of classical political economy in the years up to 1870 was such that it can be termed an ideology. The best immediate gauge of that hegemony is not to be found in the work of political economists themselves, amongst whom John Stuart Mill was perhaps the most influential, but in the breadth of reference to its principal ideas. In *Past and Present* (1843), for instance, Thomas Carlyle, despite obvious misgivings about the nature of British economic life in the 1840s and the lamentable 'condition of England'produced by it, was unable to refute the main tenets of classical political economy embodied, as he saw it, in the 'iron laws' of supply and demand set out in the 'dismal science' of David Ricardo. The hegemony of classical political economy is evident too from other contemporary texts, such as Dickens's *Hard Times* (1854) or Elizabeth Gaskell's *Mary Barton* (1848) and *North and South* (1854–5). In all of these works the consequences of economic depression are clearly seen; but similarly the economic processes which produced that state of affairs are perceived, as it were, as facts of nature; the underlying analysis of economic depression in the 1840s provided by classical political economy was never questioned in any substantial way, because, given the nature and the intellectual prestige of political economic theory at the time, such a critique was simply not possible.

The reasons for this state of affairs are not hard to find. Craufurd Goodwin has succinctly summed up political economy's intellectual dominance in the first half of the nineteenth century:

At the beginning of the 1870's the discipline of political economy had not changed markedly for nearly half a century. The subject was treated as a relatively minor part of 'moral science', consisting of certain immutable principles or laws which could be mastered easily by an unsophisticated layman after a minimum of study.[4]

Indeed the British economist William Stanley Jevons, despite the fact that he as much as anyone else was responsible for dislodging classical political economy from its position of dominance, perceived as early as 1858 the centrality of

---

[4] Craufurd Goodwin, 'Marginalism Moves', in R. D. Collison Black, A. W. Coats, and Craufurd D. W. Goodwin (eds.), *Marginal Revolution in Economics: Interpretation and Evaluation* (Durham NC, 1973), 286.

economics as the key human and social science, underwriting the epistemologies of all other allied disciplines of knowledge. The analogy he used, the relation of mathematics to the natural sciences, emphasizes that centrality:

> There are a multitude of allied branches of knowledge connected with man's condition; the relation of these to political economy is ana-logous to the connection of mechanics, astronomy, optics, sound, heat, and every other branch more or less of physical science, with pure mathematics. . . . There are plenty of people engaged with physical science, and practical science and arts may be left to look after themselves, but thoroughly to understand the principles of society appears to me now the most cogent business.[5]

And Walter Bagehot, perhaps a more reliable because less partial commentator, perceived the translation of political economy from simple economic theory into an ideology in broadly the same terms:

> Political Economy was, indeed, the favourite subject in England from about 1810 to 1840, and this to an extent which the present generation can scarcely comprehend. . . . From a short series of axioms and definitions it believed that a large part of human things, far more than is really possible, could be deduced. . . . At that time Economists indulged in happy visions; they thought the attainment of truth far easier than we have since found it to be.[6]

Bagehot elsewhere also pointed out that the 'teaching' of political economy had become so accepted that '[n]o other form of political philosophy has ever had one thousandth part of the influence on us; its teachings have settled down into the common sense of the nation, and have become irreversible.'[7] What had once been simply theoretical and practical knowledge had ossified into ideology.

However, classical political economy was not common sense at all; and neither were its doctrines irreversible. In the final three decades of the century many of the accepted orthodoxies of conventional political economy came under increasingly rigorous scrutiny. Finally they collapsed, partly under the

---

[5] *Letters and Journals of William Stanley Jevons*, ed. H. A. Jevons (London, 1886), 101.
[6] Walter Bagehot, *Economic Studies*, ed. R. Holt Hutton (1879; London, 1880), 154–7.
[7] Ibid. 1.

weight of internal contradictions, but partly too under the pressure of the theoretical critique of what is often described in economics as the marginal revolution. As a consequence, by the end of the nineteenth century the structure of economics as a discipline of knowledge, its epistemology, and its methodology were quite different from the model presented by classical political economists fifty years earlier.[8] The nature of the change from political economy to marginalism, and the reasons for it, need not detain us long; it is the consequences of that change and its paradigmatic nature which are of most immediate interest. Economic historians are generally agreed that the trigger for the decline in classical political economy was a perception of the contradictions in two of its main four tenets, the Wages Fund theory and the labour theory of value.[9] T. W. Hutchison has described the demise of these tenets in the following way:

The 1850's and 1860's saw such a great increase in population accompanied by such a palpable rise in living standards that the classical population theory, and its law of 'natural' subsistence-wages, could only in some degree be saved by putting the main emphasis on those qualifications . . . which robbed the doctrine of almost all its sting and content. . . . Once a permanent rise in working-class standards became accepted as an accomplished fact, the entire notion of a 'subsistence' level became extremely nebulous, and what might have been regarded as the one fairly firm anchor for the classical account of distribution was removed. . . . The Wages Fund doctrine was one of those aggregative macroeconomic generalizations . . . which later emerges . . . as a *non-sequitur*, or, at best, as a platitude. J. S. Mill's spectacular abandonment of the doctrine in 1869 as a 'shadow which will vanish if we go boldly up to it', was one of the more overt signs of the crumbling of the classical system.[10]

There has been a long debate among modern economic historians about the nature of the change which occurred after the publication of William Stanley Jevons's *Theory of Political Economy* in 1871 and the ensuing revolution in economic doctrines in Britain. The fundamental issue in this debate is

---

[8] See Henry Spiegel, *Growth of Economic Thought* (Englewood Cliffs, NJ, 1971), 505.
[9] The other two main tenets were population doctrine and the theory of rent. See T. W. Hutchison, *Review of Economic Doctrines 1870–1929* (Westport, Conn., 1975), 12–16.   [10] Ibid. 13.

whether Jevons's work was the cause of that revolution or merely one of many manifestations of a wholesale—and inter-national—process of intellectual change. The agency of Jevons is not my interest; the nature of the change which he brought about, or which his work articulated, none the less is, because it reveals interesting similarities to theoretical and structural changes which were taking place at the same time in other disciplines of knowledge.

Jevons graduated at London in 1865. In 1862 he had already sent to the British Association an essay, *Notice of the General Theory of Political Economy*, which anticipated in outline much of his later work. Then in 1865 he published a second work, *The Coal Question*, an account of the role of coal in the development of Britain's industrial economy. This book brought to Jevons a degree of recognition among economists, and eventually the chair of political economy at Owens College in Manchester. In 1876 Jevons left Manchester for the chair of political economy in University College, London. Ill-health forced his resignation in 1880, and in 1882, at work on his comprehensive and unfinished *Principles of Economics*, he died by drowning. His most cogent critique of the doctrines of classical political economy was in the area of labour supply. Robert B. Ekelund jun. and Robert F. Hébert have pointed out that one of the significant revisions to classical political economy which marginalism brought about was the discovery that 'the utility that an individual . . . obtains from a homogenous stock of goods is determined by the use to which the last units of the stock are put'. In so doing, marginalist economists clearly pointed out that 'the marginal utility of a stock of some particular good diminishes with increases in quantity. . . . It is the least pressing need for a commodity, not the most pressing need, that defines the exchange value of the *entire* stock of goods.'[11] Ekelund and Hébert also argue that Jevons's major innovation in economic theory was the foundation of utility analysis from which 'he constructed a theory of exchange and a theory of labor supply and capital'.[12] Jevons's arguments were based, at least in part,

---

[11] Robert B. Ekelund jun., and Robert F. Hébert, *History of Economic Theory and Method* (1975; 2nd edn., New York, 1983), 261–2.
[12] Ibid. 312.

on theories derived from physiological and utilitarian accounts of pleasure. Although such accounts of pleasure and pain had by this time become commonplace in utilitarian theory, in physiological studies, and—as I shall suggest in the following chapter—in some aesthetic theories, Jevons's appropriation of them for economics was quite novel. Marginal utility theory defined economic choice in terms of pleasure and pain, considered not as general categories but *individually*:

A unit of pleasure or of pain is difficult even to conceive; but it is the amount of these feelings which is continually prompting us to buying and selling, borrowing and lending, labouring and resting, producing and consuming; and *it is from the quantitative effects of the feelings that we must estimate their comparative amounts.*[13]

It is worth noting that similar lines of argument occur in many otherwise unrelated disciplines of Victorian thought. Indeed, Ekelund and Hébert have gone so far as to suggest that this change in the manner in which the concept of value was understood in economic theory clearly relates to changes in contemporary thinking about human motives in general, and about pleasure in particular:

Jevons asserted that maximizing pleasure is the object of economics or, in his own words, humans seek to procure the 'greatest amount of what is desirable at the expense of the least that is undesirable'. . . . [Jevons's] theory of marginal utility is basically simple and straight-forward. . . . [He] clearly specified that a utility function is a relation between the commodities an individual consumes and an act of individual valuation. Utility is not, in sum, an *intrinsic* or inherent quality that things possess. Instead, utility has meaning only in the act of valuation. . . . *Jevons's law* may then be stated as follows: The degree of utility for a single commodity varies with the quantity possessed of that commodity and ultimately decreases as the quantity of that single commodity increases.[14]

As I have indicated earlier, some historians of economic thought have seen at work here much larger forces than those endogenous to economics alone. Underneath these marginalist

---

[13] William Stanley Jevons, *Theory of Political Economy* (1871; London, 1957), 11. Quoted in Ekelund and Hébert, *Economic Theory and Method*, 313.
[14] Ibid. 314–15.

revisions to the theory of value, or in some way motivating them, Lawrence Birken has detected profound changes in epistemology. In his view, what marked out the marginalist revolution was a change so fundamental that it reversed the traditional characterization of economic activity as an aspect of 'productivism', the view that production was the ultimate end of economic activity. Birken suggests that the marginalists 'started with the assumption that human beings were first of all *consumers* . . . [and explained] how consumers were provisioned by the economy'. Up to 1870 'the *primary focus* had always been productivist in the sense that individual consumption was subordinated to ongoing macroeconomic considerations. Now, these values were decidedly inverted. Where the focus had been on the economy as a whole, the new stress was on how the economy might provision the individual.'[15] Such a change involved, according to Birken, a dramatic revaluation of how economics, as an intellectual discipline, was situated in relation to other disciplines of knowledge. In particular the theoretical revisions in economics drew upon a changed concept of the individual:

From the seventeenth to the nineteenth century, classical social theorists had tended to see society as a *reflex* of the economic; in the late nineteenth and twentieth century, marginalism reversed this hierarchy of values so that the economic now became the reflex of the psychological. In other words, the economic gradually ceased to understand itself as the autonomous center of social life and instead constituted itself simply as a means of satisfying individual psychologies.[16]

Some of the attacks on classical political economy in the decades following the marginal revolution bear out Birken's

---

[15] Birken, *From Macroeconomics to Microeconomics*, 253–4.

[16] Ibid. 258. But cf. E. K. Hunt, *History of Economic Thought: A Critical Perspective* (Belmont, Calif., 1979), who argues that towards the end of the nineteenth century the nature of capitalism changed and industrial capitalists became finance capitalists. In Hunt's view the labour theory of value proposed by classical political economy lost its appeal in this transition, and marginalism provided the appropriate ideological justification for financial capitalism. Mark Blaug suggests political reasons for the success of marginalism, and argues that marginalism was an essential and required balance to Marxism and Fabian thought—in other words that it was a political necessity. See Blaug, 'Was there a Marginal Revolution?', in Black, Coats, and Goodwin (eds.), *Marginal Revolution in Economics*, 305–20.

observation precisely because they questioned the assumptions about human nature which classical political economy had used. Interestingly, these speculations were to be tested by the infant discipline of economic history, for historical research allowed the assumptions of political economy to be tested empirically. In fact, social philosophers and economic historians—such as Cliffe Leslie and Arnold Toynbee—considered an examination of the epistemology of political economy to be one of their most pressing tasks. Toynbee went as far as to declare that 'the society dominated by an economic man was a figment of Ricardo's fertile imagination'. Gerard M. Koot has suggested that this doubt about the epistemology of political economy was at the heart of Toynbee's dissatisfaction with it:

[Toynbee] argued that the deductive method of classical political economy was possible only if the 'economic man' was a true reflection of psychological motivation. Toynbee explained that only an inductive study of economics would . . . take a broader view of the psychological makeup of man.[17]

Towards the end of the century, marginalist economics became dominant within the profession and effectively superseded classical political economy. The most important consequence of the demise of some of the tenets of classical political economy was the accompanying demise of its pretensions to explain human behaviour; thus marginalism, originally a narrowly conceived body of economic theory, in effect undermined classical political economy's status as an ideology. There were several components involved in that decline. At the endogeneous level, there was nothing in economics explained by classical political economy which could not be more cogently and more elegantly explained by marginalism; and there were some problems of economic explanation omitted by classical political economy which *could* be accounted for by marginalism. However, changes at the exogenous level had far greater implications. The revolution brought about by marginal analysis involved redefining some of the epistemological assumptions upon which economic doctrines had hitherto rested; and it did so in order to take account of elements of other nineteenth-

[17] Gerard M. Koot, 'English Historical Economics and the Emergence of Economic History in England', *History of Political Economy*, 12 (1980), 187.

century disciplines of knowledge. This, at the most fundamental level, involved invoking a model of human activity and human nature in many ways opposed to that inherent in the epistemology of classical political economy. Classical political economy could no longer propose a model of human behaviour which claimed to explain the totality of human actions. Hence the most profound change which political economy underwent was an epistemological one, the main consequence of which was that it became simply one of many competing explanations of human behaviour—and a discredited one at that. The changes which the marginal revolution brought about coincided with and, perhaps to some extent caused, a change in assumptions about human motivation similar to epistemological changes occurring simultaneously in other disciplines of knowledge. As I shall point out below, the career of political economy as a discipline of thought coincided with changes in historiography, in sociology, and in psychology. These changes had two elements; one involved the nature of authority within a discipline—the grounds, that is, upon which one explanation was preferred to competing explanations; and the other involved the epistemological status of the discipline itself—how, and in what ways it derived its explanatory power.

The marginal revolution also coincided with—and again perhaps was one of the causes of—the accelerating professionalization, specialization, and institutionalization of economics within an academic environment. In these senses, too, the development of the discipline of economics in the late nineteenth century is paradigmatic. The 1870s was a decade when economists were acutely aware of the future of their subject.[18] Economics as a purely academic discipline (as opposed to its status as an ideology) was held in particularly low esteem in the 1860s. The history of academic economic thought is one which is generally characterized in terms of its methodological uncertainty. A. W. Coats has pointed out that economics was (and is) a 'discipline in which the criteria of valid knowledge have been difficult to define and to apply, and

---

[18] See John Maloney, *Marshall, Orthodoxy and the Professionalisation of Economics* (Cambridge, 1985), 7–21.

in which ideological and other non-logical influences have been highly influential'.[19] Coats sees this as particularly true of the first half of the nineteenth century, when economics, as an academic discipline of knowledge, was subordinate to other disciplines, such as moral philosophy, and when this subordination was reflected both in the number of academic posts given to the subject by British universities, and in the prestige of the subject among undergraduates. In the early years of the nineteenth century, despite the large set of shared assumptions of its practitioners, economics was neither a professional, nor an institutionalized, discipline of knowledge. Debates about economics were not restricted to a subgroup: figures as varied as the politician W. E. Gladstone, the philosopher Henry Sidgwick, the Comtean sociologist Frederic Harrison, and the historian Walter Bagehot, all felt free to claim authority and to write copiously on the subject. In all these cases authority did not reside within an institution, nor in an appeal made to either a specialized body of knowledge or to a community of specialists. Rather, it was the prestige of the individual concerned, or the prestige brought from other areas of intellectual activity, which gave authority to individual statements about economics. This particular feature of academic debate in economics frequently recurs in the middle years of the nineteenth century. Certainly in his strictures about the 'dead hand' and 'noxious influence' of intellectual orthodoxy, Jevons complained that authority in contemporary economic argument *did not derive* from any internal logic or empirical evidence. He identified John Stuart Mill as a figure whose immense personal prestige lent authority to statements which, in Jevons's view, were not *in themselves intellectually coherent.* The example of Mill is the most famous, but it is not the only one: Gladstone's statements about economics, for instance, derived their authority simply from his prestige as a politician. (It is amusing to note that since 1870, from this very diverse group of laymen, only prime ministers have continued to arrogate to themselves the authority to speak on such a specialized subject as economics.)

[19] A. W. Coats, 'The Role of Authority in the Development of British Economics', *Journal of Law and Economics*, 7 (1964), 86.

In reaction to this state of affairs, economists during the 1870s identified two ambitions for their subject. The first was that it should become more rigorous; in this respect Jevons's view, that economics should imitate the rigour of the natural sciences, was not an untypical one. The second ambition was that economics should seek the sort of prestige which would allow it to intervene in matters of policy. (This feature of a burgeoning professionalization, which demanded the combination of theoretical rigour and specialist knowledge, is, as I shall point out, one that is repeated in the contemporary history of many other disciplines of knowledge.) John Maloney has identified the three main criteria whereby professionalization in economics may be assessed: a specialized body of theory, an effective monopoly of a defined specialist function, and the observation of professional ethics sanctioned by institutional or peer-group pressure.[20] Necessarily then, professionalization along these lines had to take place principally within universities. In his description of the history of economics after the marginal revolution, T. W. Hutchison emphasizes precisely this point:

Economic theory was to be rebuilt mainly by university economists, by men who specialized much more thoroughly than their mainly non-academic predecessors—financiers, journalists, and civil servants. . . . Standards of rigour and precision in the formulation of pure theory, or rather in the superstructure thereof[,] . . . were to be higher, beyond all recognition, than ever before, and progress in this respect was to be unprecedentedly rapid.[21]

Indeed, the process became self-reinforcing. Economists working on marginal utility theory were predominantly academics; moreover, the theory itself placed a special emphasis upon generality and upon scholarship, and both these factors ensured the restriction of economic debate to an academic environment.[22] The specialization of economics led to its professionalization; and professionalization in its turn reinforced that specialization.

If my argument that after the 1870s writing on economics

[20] Maloney, *Marshall*, 3.

[21] Hutchison, *Review of Economic Doctrines*, 30–1.

[22] See George J. Stigler, 'Adoption of the Marginal Utility Theory', in Black, Coats, and Goodwin (eds.), *Marginal Revolution in Economics*, 305–20.

became a specialized matter is correct, then it must also hold for many other disciplines of thought—for history, sociology, psychology, and so forth. For example, art critics and literary critics, such as John Ruskin, could write freely on economics or politics in the 1860s, but could *not* do so in the 1880s. Specialization extended to all disciplines of knowledge, including literary criticism; hence the nature of literary criticism was affected by what was happening within universities. Figures such as Benjamin Jowett and John Campbell Shairp, with the immense authority of the institutions in which they worked, became increasingly influential in deciding the character of academic critical discourse.

But there were other consequences of the professionalization of economics in the last decades of the nineteenth century; and these also have interesting analogues in other contemporary disciplines. As I have noted, in the last two decades of the nineteenth century the new specialism of the *history* of economics came about. The emergence of a general 'scientific' historiography in the nineteenth century was accompanied by a demand for a widespread and increased historical understanding of contemporary issues.[23] As a consequence, an emphasis upon a properly documented and empirically verifiable economic history coincided with the emergence of marginalism as the dominant theory within economics. The growth of the role of history in economic studies had two functions: it redefined the concept of the 'economic', in the process bringing to the surface some of the hitherto hidden assumptions of classical political economy; and it allowed the theoretical speculation of the present to be tested against the evidence of the past. Gerard M. Koot has characterized the 'historical school' of the time as a 'body of criticism . . . which promoted the study of economic history and applied economics'.[24] The principal figures, amongst whom Cliffe Leslie and J. E. Thorold Rogers were the best known, were able to question theoretical orthodoxy at an empirical level. Consequently Leslie and Rogers could confirm the recent theoretical speculations of Jevons by insisting that, for example, Ricardo's theory of wages had not been true for

---

[23] See Koot, 'English Historical Economics', 176.
[24] Ibid. 179.

any period in the past, and was thus not likely to be true of the present either.[25]

None the less, the fundamental area of disagreement of economic historians with classical political economy was once more at the epistemological level. According to early economic historians, the concept of human nature which had under-written classical political economy was simply inadequate to the demands made of it. Koot describes Leslie's attack in 1876 upon the classical assumption of the 'economic man' as, in the first instance, an epistemological critique:

Historical study, Leslie argued, demonstrated that man was not a being who moved society through a 'desire for wealth'; but instead, was a complex organism ruled by 'passions, appetites, affections, moral and religious sentiments, family feelings, aesthetical tastes and intellectual wants'. Further, orthodox economics had also distorted economic conclusions by an excessive emphasis upon the individual, while, in reality, 'the conclusion which the study of society makes every day more irresistible is that the germ from which the existing economy of every nation has been evolved is not the individual, still less the personification of an abstraction, but the primitive community'.[26]

The dissatisfaction, then, with the model of classical political economy, among both the new economic historians and the marginalists, was at heart a dissatisfaction with its assumptions about human nature. Thus Leslie could in passing allude to the newly invented disciplines of sociology, psychology, and anthropology. Each of these disciplines of knowledge invoked a notion of human nature which was defined by means of bio-logical metaphors or biological paradigms. Within sociology and psychology the 'appetites and affections' described by Leslie became central concepts. And as human beings were defined by reference to biological analogies, so too, ultimately, were human societies. Contemporary critiques of political economy expressed the same kind of dissatisfaction with it as those earlier in the century had done (in, for example, *Past and Present*); but by the 1880s and the 1890s, the crucial difference

---

[25] Koot, 'English Historical Economics', 184–5.
[26] Ibid. 181–2. Koot is quoting Cliffe Leslie, 'On the Philosophical Method of Political Economy', in id., *Essays in Philosophy* (London, 1876), 230.

lay in the ability of the marginalist to demonstrate theoretical inadequacy of political economy, and in the ability of the historian to demonstrate its historical inaccuracy.

To sum up briefly, then. In the decades following 1871 the critique of classical political economy as an economic theory also brought about its demise as an ideology. This ideological decline resulted in a crisis of intellectual authority. In so far as it had appeared to embody 'truths' about human nature, political economy embodied the dominant form of intellectual authority. But after the marginal revolution it became only one source of authority among many competitors. Moreover, the inadequacy of the theoretical base of political economy was accompanied by and partly precipitated the rise of economic history as a discipline of knowledge which offered the possibility of the empirical testing of theory.

2. HISTORIOGRAPHY

The most striking feature of the history of historiography in the nineteenth century also involves the problems of authority and epistemology. Moreover, the period when questions about the status of historiography were focused most sharply coincides precisely with the moment of crisis in political economy which I have described above.

For the purposes of this study, nineteenth-century British historiography can be tentatively divided into three periods. The first half of the century was dominated by the personalities and work of Macaulay and Carlyle, 'amateur' historians who embodied the prevailing early nineteenth-century view of the historian as a gentleman rather than an expert or scholar. 1857 marked the beginning of the middle period of controversy when these assumptions were threatened by the publication of Henry Buckle's *History of Civilization in England*. The ensuing debate, which lasted well into the late 1880s, was over the nature and methods of what was to be the new 'scientific' historiography. Buckle had argued for a materialist, abstract history which took as its premiss the presupposition that all human behaviour, like the physical world, was governed by regular principles or laws; he maintained that without the assumption that human behaviour was determined, history could not generalize, and therefore could not be scientific. As matters turned out, however, the dominant group among British historians preferred the new German tradition of scholarship, concentrating, as it did, on facts, on the minute critical examination of archives and sources. The final period from the 1890s onwards (one with which this study is only glancingly concerned) saw the establishment of the German model as the new orthodoxy of historical explanation.

It is generally accepted that British historiography throughout the nineteenth century was dominated by the Whiggish principle of gradualism.[27] The hegemony of Whig historiography is usually traced back to its influential interpretation of the Glorious Revolution of 1688. Whig historiography astutely combined two contrary traditions of the historiography of revolution into one new interpretation: that of providential history. In this history, the Glorious Revolution marked an important moment in a continuing evolution of English liberties: moreover, it both affirmed and guaranteed those liberties for the future.[28] The Whig interpretation of history seemed to offer an especially felicitous reconciliation of past, present and future.[29] And it was this tradition which Macaulay inherited and which he, more than any other contemporary figure, popularized. J. W. Burrow has noted how:

The history of England was that of a deeply, almost, it seemed, providentially favoured country; favoured by circumstance, by the spirit of its people and institutions from an early date, and by its history. In constitutional essentials England was qualified to be the tutor, not the pupil, of a more distracted world. This, in outline and in much of its detail, was the version of English history inherited by Macaulay, and displayed by him with all the imaginative energy of a copious, unperplexed mind.[30]

Burrow goes on to suggest that Macaulay rewrote English history to create periods of public life which were recognizably traditional, humanistic, and Whig, as well as being intensely individualistic. Indeed, Macaulay was famous for the indi-

---

[27] See Hedva Ben-Israel, *Historians on the French Revolution* (Cambridge, 1968).

[28] See J. W. Burrow, *Liberal Descent: Victorians and the English Past* (Cambridge, 1981).

[29] See Ernst Breisach, *Historiography: Ancient, Medieval and Modern* (Chicago, Ill., 1983).

[30] Burrow, *Liberal Descent*, 35.

viduality of his style, and an idiosyncrasy of treatment which gave the past a new relevance and accessibility. In 1828 he had characterized history in a way which emphasized its literary qualities: 'History, at least in its state of ideal perfection, is a compound of poetry and philosophy.'[31] There were very good reasons why Macaulay's 'literary' historiography was so successful. As T. W. Heyck has argued, Macaulay's work met the needs of an early nineteenth-century literate public. Whig historiography used the past as a guide through the present, and thus it provided a ground for hope that change would be beneficial. And in order to reach a wide audience for this providential interpretation of history, Macaulay paid careful attention to what modern historiographers would call the 'literary' aspects of its written character—its narrative elements and its style, that is. The emphasis was on individual agency—and thus history was conceived as a species of drama with the major figures of the past characterized as either heroes or villains. History became the assertion of the autonomy of the individual against vast impersonal forces of materialism and political revolution. And in this respect it is significant that British interpretations of the French Revolution for the most part rejected the historiography of writers such as Thiers and Mignet on the grounds that Revolutionary historiography, through the attribution of historical change to ideas or abstract forces, denied to the individual any moral agency—a qualification which recurs in British reactions to Comtean sociology.

None of the early and mid-Victorian writers of history were historians in the sense that we would understand the term today; none saw the discovery of new information about the past as an end in itself; none gave priority to the critical examination of source-material.[32] But matters changed radically in the middle of the century. By the early 1860s Macaulay's history had become discredited for several reasons. The main

---

[31] Quoted in T. W. Heyck, *Transformation of Intellectual Life in Victorian England* (London, 1982), 122.

[32] Nevertheless, two groups of historians liked to think of themselves as 'scientific'. They were, on the one hand, J. S. Mill and George Grote, successors of the Rationalists —Hume, Robertson, and Ferguson; and on the other the Liberal Anglicans—Thomas Arnold, Richard Whatley, J. C. Hare, Connop Thirwall, H. H. Hillman, and J. P. Stanley; these wished to see each period and each nation's history having its own 'spirit'.

cause of the decline in his reputation was the introduction into Britain of new German critical standards of historical scholarship and a new intellectual rigour in determining the nature of evidence. Macaulay had written without knowledge of these standards, and his history, when tested by them, was found to be deficient. By 1860 then, it was clear that Macaulay's historiography was neither relevant nor authoritative. Both a new historical subject, and a new and a more scientific or scholarly historiography were necessary.

There was, moreover, another challenge to the concept of individual agency; for it was recognized that there might be other criteria involved in explaining human history. The crisis in historiography, then, was not merely a simple one concerning the status and nature of evidence; at issue also was the nature of historical *explanation*, and the grounds upon which those explanations were to be justified. This in essence was the challenge of Henry Buckle's concept of abstract materialism. Buckle's *History of Civilization in England*, published between 1857 (volume i) and 1861 (volume ii), began a debate about the scientific status of history. His contribution to that debate was important but it was negative: for though his work was taken to be the prime example of what a scientific historiography should *not* be, he nevertheless forced other historians to debate what it should be. Buckle's positivist history was indebted to several figures; but most controversially to the French sociologist Auguste Comte and to the statistician Adolphe Quetelet. In the case of Comte the extent of his influence over Buckle is the subject of debate among modern historians, but it is none the less true that many of Buckle's contemporary critics were convinced that he and Comte were alike in propagandizing an impersonal, irreligious history. And hence much of the criticism of his work derived from the general hostility, especially in clerical circles, directed against Auguste Comte.[33]

Human society for Buckle was not to be considered as the totality of individual actants but as an abstract entity; and Buckle's aim, to discover the laws of human progress, was undertaken through the examination of statistics, particularly

---

[33] See T. R. Wright, *Religion of Humanity* (Cambridge, 1986), 158–63.

of murders and suicides. He attempted to prove that what were generally called 'random' events (such as suicides) had an underlying regularity and hence an identifiable social cause. The argument behind his general theory of causation was as follows: food depends upon climate; wealth and population upon food; and civilization derives from wealth:

[N]othing is casual or accidental; and the whole march of affairs is governed by general causes, which, owing to their largeness and remoteness, often escape attention, but which, when once recognised, are found to be marked by a simplicity and uniformity, which are the invariable characteristics of the highest truths that the mind of man has reached.[34]

Buckle endeavoured to revise the nature of historical explanation in the sense that he wished to see the concept of human agency subject to abstract generalization. Human beings might exist in time, and therefore all human action could be said to be unique; but the laws, the material causation, which circumscribed and thus partly determined those actions, had an atemporal existence. The controversy in historiography brought about by Buckle's work was at heart a fundamental contradiction between social explanations which emphasized the temporal, and therefore unrepeatable, nature of human actions, and those which saw human action governed by processes not in themselves subject to temporal change. I shall return to this contradiction in my discussion of British sociology.

Buckle's historiography was criticized on several counts. One of the primary objections was to his reductively deterministic model of man and to his materialist laws of causation. These, it was alleged, ran counter to the English tradition of free will, moral agency and individualism. And along with these changes went accusations of anticlericalism, for Buckle allegedly denied the role of Providence in the course of history. Moreover, Buckle's open contempt for the scholarship of Cambridge and Oxford also made him enemies. In the first volume of his *History* he began with an attack on Oxford as 'that ancient University, which had always been esteemed as the

---

[34] Henry Buckle, *History of Civilization in England* (London, 1872), iii. 19.

refuge of superstition'.[35] And, as Giles St Aubyn points out, he was in turn accused by them of being a dilettante:

The hostility Buckle provoked was admittedly of his own making, for his criticism was always outspoken and many reviewers had injuries to avenge. Oxford and Cambridge, at the time when he wrote, were still predominantly clerical, and thus his contempt for their scholarship and his attacks on many of their most cherished dogmas, scarcely inclined them to charity. Both the Church and the Universities resented what they regarded as outrageous slander poured upon them by a mere dilettante, who believed he could educate himself, and who actually dared to challenge their monopoly of wisdom and learning.[36]

Other criticism was more specific: Lord Acton deprecated Buckle's excessive reliance on statistical evidence; William Stubbs and Charles Darwin his emphasis on the masses rather than on the individual. In his entry on Buckle in the *Dictionary of National Biography*, Leslie Stephen attributed his many faults to his lack of a university education. There were also more general attacks on Buckle's methodology made by the tactic of criticizing the French sociologist Auguste Comte, with whom, as we have seen, he was associated. A representative figure in this respect was Charles Kingsley who, in his inaugural lecture at Cambridge in 1860 entitled 'The Limits of Exact Science as Applied to History', attacked the fashion for philosophies of history produced by French models of historiography and by the influence of the inductive sciences. While accepting the principles of 'order and progress' he felt that history belonged to moral rather than to 'positivist sciences': human history came about through the action of great individuals inspired by God.[37]

The principal point to be made here is that the issues which have been identified in the development of political economy in the nineteenth century recurred in the controversies about

---

[35] See Giles St Aubyn, *Victorian Eminence: The Life and Works of Henry Buckle* (London, 1958), 5.

[36] Ibid. 163.

[37] There were also partial criticisms from W. E. H. Lecky in his *History of the Rise and Influence of the Spirit of Rationalism in Europe* (2 vols., London, 1865); and more generally there was Arnold's dismissal of the Comteans in *Culture and Anarchy* in 1869. See also Thomas Huxley, 'Scientific Aspects of Positivism', *Fortnightly Review*, 11 (1869), 653–70, which referred disparagingly to Positivism and to Comte.

historiography. Arguments about the logic of explanation of social phenomena became confused with what gave explanations their authority: in the terms which I used earlier to characterize the evolution of political economy, the endogenous and the exogenous interacted. The rejection of Buckle's historiography owed more to the fact that he possessed no institutional authority for his views than to allegations of their internal incoherence. Buckle, in a way strangely reminiscent of Jevons (and, as I shall suggest, the literary critic John Churton Collins) was placed outside academic and intellectual orthodoxies. Both men were to a certain extent motivated by their very heterodoxy. But a consequence of that heterodoxy was that issues which could have been resolved solely on the basis of the logic of intellectual explanation became confused with questions of the prestige of their proponents. In the end, Jevons's work was instrumental in founding a new orthodoxy; Buckle's was not.

While a scientific history was not to be based on Buckle's materialist methodology, the idea of scientific rigour was not abandoned. (In fact, as I shall argue later, the antagonism between advocates of a history derived from sociology and a history dependent upon archives was motivated by a profound disagreement over epistemology.) T. R. Wright has argued that there was some very partial support for Comte among Cambridge historians other than Kingsley, although it was limited to accepting the currency of his phrases rather than the implications of his theory.[38] There was, moreover, fairly widespread support, especially in the 1870s and 1880s, for the general idea that history should have a scientific basis. However, the model for this scientific history was to be found in German rather than French scholarship. In a lecture in Oxford in 1877, William Stubbs, one of the figures most instrumental in bringing about the new standards of rigour and scholarship in historiography in Britain in the 1870s and 1880s, stated the objections to the concept of history as an exact science, not in terms of theoretical inadequacy, but simply in terms of pragmatics; it failed to do any work for the practising historian:

---

[38] See T. R. Wright, *Religion of Humanity*, 160.

Shall I be saying too much if I say at once that one great objection to the very idea of reducing History to the lines and rules of exact science lies in the fact . . . that generalizations become obscurer and more useless as they grow wider, and, as they grow narrower and more special, cease to have any value as generalizations at all? Is not a historical science liable, if it can be elaborated at all, to become on the one hand a mere table of political formulae and on the other a case-book of political casuistry? . . . And is not the fact that the idea of a science of History finds acceptance, not among practical historians, but among high-paced theorists, a proof that such a possibility belongs to theory and not to practice?[39]

The problem of the nature of intellectual authority was also one addressed by Stubbs. The idea of intellectual authority residing in the prestige of the individual was perceived in the 1860s as being no longer tenable, but there was no clearly defined alternative. Writing in the 1870s, Stubbs was able to suggest that the relationship between individual prestige and the authority of evidence had been misunderstood. He discussed authority in Carlyle's work by asking:

Shall I be thought hard if I say that the popularity of Carlyle's Frederick was not an intelligent appreciation; that it was Carlyle's reputation and manner that made men read it; and that it was for the Carlyle not the Frederick that they cared whilst they wholly missed the prophet's lesson?[40]

A year later he returned to the subject of the relationship between the authority of evidence or data and the prestige of the individual historian:

Of course it may be said that a great deal of useless knowledge is accumulated in this way; what good can be done, it may be said, by analysing Matthew Paris, and determining how much of his narrative is drawn from ancient charters, or foreign letters, lives of saints, or such stribiligines: it is his historic power and authority that gives them value, not they that give authority to him. Not quite so, I think, and even if it were so, there might be a lesson in the mere proof of the fact; the analysis is necessary for the due estimate of his value as a historian; the writer who can pass such an ordeal where it is possible to apply it, may be trusted where it is not possible to apply it.[41]

[39] William Stubbs, *Seventeen Lectures and Addresses on the Study of Medieval and Modern History and Kindred Subjects* (1886; 3rd edn., Oxford, 1900), 103.
[40] Ibid. 68–9.   [41] Ibid. 92.

The 1870s and 1880s witnessed a gradual acceptance of German historiography by British historians. Leopold von Ranke, whom Stubbs had called 'beyond all comparison the greatest historical scholar alive [and] . . . one of the greatest historians that ever lived', had laid an emphasis upon facts and on the meticulous examination of sources.[42] Arguments for such methodological precision had been given added impetus by the success of the new science of epigraphy; B. G. Niebuhr and Theodor Mommsen, for example, had used the corpus of Roman inscriptions to reconstruct Roman history. However, it was Stubbs and Edward Freeman who were finally responsible for the transformation of British historiography according to the German model, and for instituting history as an academic discipline. This new view of the role of historical scholarship and the practice of history had several important consequences. It changed the status of the historian, because historical knowledge was now considered to be cumulative and hence the individual scholar was seen to be contributing only a small part to the totality of historical knowledge. And accompanying this change was the notion of a scholarly community—residing in the university—in whose collective judgement historical authority was now perceived to reside.[43] However, more than these specific points, general questions about the relevance of evidence, what was to count as evidence in history, what indeed was to count as history, as we shall see, all had direct implications for the development of *literary* history, a subject which, with the professionalization of literary studies, was—in a formal context at least—'new' in the 1880s and 1890s.

3. SOCIOLOGY

The crises in British historiography described above have a compelling symmetry with those in British sociology. As I have indicated, British historiography in the years between 1855 and

[42] Ibid. 65.

[43] Stephen Bann has also noted another change brought about by Ranke's insistence on facts and the distinction between imagination and invention—a new historical poetics: a call to repress the rhetorical status of historical writing which had been a common feature of it in the eighteenth century. See Stephen Bann, *Clothing of Clio: A Study of the Representation of History in Nineteenth-Century Britain and France* (Cambridge, 1984).

1880 rejected an epistemology which sought explanations derived from general laws of abstract causation and tended instead to endorse explanations which emphasized the particularity (and hence the uniqueness) of historical events. In broad terms, it was these same controversies which were at issue in the development of sociology as a discipline: the crises in historiography and sociology, in whatever surface terms they were characterized at the time, were fundamentally those of epistemology. And in sociology the epistemological challenge was posed by the systematizing tendency of Comtean thought.

The conflict between British empirical historiography on the one hand, and Comtean and Spencerian sociology on the other, has been described by Kenneth Bock in *The Acceptance of Histories* (1956). Bock sees the antagonism between the two disciplines in the middle decades of the nineteenth century in purely epistemological terms—it derived from an incompatibility in the explanations of human behaviour which each discipline invoked. Bock discusses the emergence of the social sciences, and particularly of sociology, as discrete disciplines of knowledge in the mid-nineteenth century as scientific, but none the less historical, explanations of society which were in competition with accepted explanations of the same phenomena provided by academic historians. Historians working within British traditions of historiography undertook to produce 'faithful representations of detailed, concrete, time-and-place events in the experiences of particular people'.[44] Traditional historiography could not be accommodated into any new science of society, because it held that historical evidence, being specific to a time and a place, was unique; and if unique, unrepeatable; and if unrepeatable, by definition incapable of being brought into the domain of scientific verifiability. The methods of explanation in the social sciences required a different concept of the historical. Bock goes on to suggest that the opposition between sociology, anthropology, and psychology on the one hand, and accepted historiography on the other, was in fact derived from a fundamental opposition of what society was perceived to be. In particular, some aspects of these models of human society were not just in opposition, but violently so; and thus disagreements over what was to count as evidence,

---

[44] Kenneth Bock, *Acceptance of Histories* (Berkeley, Calif., 1956), 16.

authority, and proof in these disciplines was fundamentally a disagreement about epistemology. In Comtean theories of sociology or in Spencerian theories of psychology, explanations of social structures were accounts which invoked a biological or a physical metaphor: societies or nations were constituted in the manner of an organism: they evolved, they flourished, they decayed, and then they died. The general currents of nineteenth-century British historiography, on the other hand, stressed the uniqueness and autonomy of the individual act. History was constituted by individual acts and individual actants, both of which could be located within a specific, and not necessarily repeatable, historical sequence, amenable to investigation through documentary or archival evidence. It is within this context that Bock places the use made by nineteenth-century sociologists, psychologists, and anthropologists of biological or physiological analogies:

> The seemingly curious decision of a Ferguson or a Comte to seek generalizations about man's experience by ignoring the particulars to which those generalizations must refer is intimately connected with the Aristotelian dictum that there is an order of human actions that are not in nature, are inexplicable in terms of natural causes, and hence cannot be made the subject of scientific study. The early modern effort to establish a historical science of man rests squarely on the persistent notions that historical events are unique, that science does not deal with the unique, and that a science of history must therefore weave a circuitous route around its proper subject matter. . . . The biological analogy, the idea of progress, . . . evolutionism, the doctrine of survivals . . . assume importance only when the resolve to seek generalizations about temporal process is accompanied by the conviction that the detailed record of temporal process cannot be utilized for such a purpose.[45]

Sociology organized on a Comtean basis in fact failed to take root in Britain. And that failure had both an epistemological and an institutional cause. The institutional constraints, in so far as they had their origins in university structures, were irrelevant, for sociology never established itself within British universities in the nineteenth century. British intellectual activity was intimately involved with the political, ecclesiastical,

---

[45] Ibid. 85–6.

and social élites of the country, and their interests effectively excluded sociological thinking. The only way in which nineteenth-century sociology could be professionalized was by affiliating itself to the machinery of government. Effectively, the only professional role which sociology could play was that of a determinant of social policy. For sociology to emerge as a discrete area of intellectual activity required the transformation of existing epistemologies, for the primary pre-condition for sociological thought was a fundamental doubt about the very premiss of society. But in Britain that pre-social epistemology had a peculiarly firm institutional hold. However, in France the analytic sociology of Comte was already firmly established, because the French Revolution had made necessary some kind of theoretical analysis of the very nature or structure of the new society which it had brought into existence; whereas in Britain, where historiography had alienated the concept of revolution from British history, and valorized instead constitutional continuity, there were no such corresponding doubts. Indeed the impetus was in the opposite direction: towards a complacency which took for granted one single concept of society. Social ills were perceived only as social problems requiring cosmetic changes or piecemeal reforms which did not challenge the underlying structure of society. Thus British society was immune from sociological enquiry in a way which French society was not.

What characterized the Comtean intellectual tradition was its rationalist, deductive, and monist systems of thought rather than the empiricist and inductive methods operating in Britain.[46] British social thinking, in a manner similar to historiographical speculation, took as its model of authority the individual: there was no collective authority, such as the church, the monarchy, or the state, which demanded submission. Nor was there a corresponding *belief* in such an overarching principle, only in the notion of a variety of causes, effects, and futures, each changing according to circumstances. These conflicting ideologies necessarily gave rise to different sorts of social and sociological thought. As a consequence, social science became reduced to matters of facts and figures

---

[46] See Geoffrey Hawthorn, *Enlightenment and Despair: A History of Social Theory* (1976; 2nd edn., Cambridge, 1987), 8–14.

—to the domain of the famous Victorian Blue Books: the governmental enquiries and statistical surveys which made those books possible were derived from (and in their turn strengthened the base of) British traditions of empirical research. Once more the methodological importance of the provision of verifiable historical knowledge links developments in sociology with those in historiography. When in the 1870s—for the first time in the century—social and economic conditions *did* result in a crisis of ideology, one of the consequences of the ensuing debate over the function and direction of the human and social sciences was the firm rejection of French analytic thought in favour of empirical sociology.[47]

Now at about the same time as these crises of authority in political economy, historiography, and sociology, as following chapters will make clear, literary and art criticism in Britain underwent similar far-reaching changes. Critical authority, hitherto seen as residing in the prestige of the individual —recall Mill's description of himself to Carlyle in 1833— became progressively less easy to define. Increasingly both literary and art criticism became the province of an academic and intellectual establishment; critical practices, hitherto unsystematic and 'amateur', became institutionalized. As with social science, and particularly economics, different, and at times quite contradictory, epistemologies were sought by critics to justify critical practices. At the same time the increasing institutionalization of literary studies within universities moved the source of authority from the individual, who up to then could authorize a judgement simply by virtue of his prestige, to the group, for whom judgements were valid only in so far as they were *collectively* acceptable. Moreover, as they became a collective responsibility, so they were endorsed by the general paraphernalia of scholarship which had already been valorized in disciplines such as history and the history of economics. So academic literary and art criticism tended to borrow from those other disciplines principles for validating its judgements and its procedures: academic literary study also became historical—began to use literary history, that is—and

[47] For the consequences of the collapse of the ideology of political economy, see Stefan Collini, Donald Winch, and John Burrow, *That Noble Science of Politics: A Study in Nineteenth-Century Intellectual History* (Cambridge, 1983).

thus began to use archival and empirical research. Literature was perceived as possessing a history which could be systematically described; and its texts could be scrutinized with the same rigour as the texts of theology or history. Critics outside such institutions, and hence unable to employ these and similar principles of authority, tended, as in the past, to see authority still residing in the individual. After the 1870s, however, the prestige of such critics diminished, and their work became increasingly marginal. None the less the persistent attempts by writers, particularly those associated with the Aesthetic Movement, still to define critical authority in terms of individual prestige was not without some considerable intellectual justification. While the epistemology which guaranteed the authority of a burgeoning British literary history was ultimately that of British historiography, with its renewed emphasis upon source and archival evidence, the competing discipline of knowledge which underwrote many of the individual critics of the Aesthetic Movement was that of psychology.

The relevance of all this is easy to see if it is set against the reception of two of the most notorious critical texts of the 1870s and 1880s, Walter Pater's *Studies in the History of the Renaissance* (1873) and Edmund Gosse's *From Shakespeare to Pope* (1885).[48] Both works created a public controversy, but in each instance the nature of the controversy was quite different, partly because, as I have shown, the nature of critical authority was itself changing. Pater's book was attacked when it was first published; indeed, between 1873 and 1876, when Pater was the subject of scandal and blackmail at Oxford and subsequently failed to obtain the election for the Professorship of Poetry, *The Renaissance* endured 'a torrent of rebuke from religious and conservative circles in Oxford'.[49] The criticism was directed at

[48] The full title of Gosse's work is *From Shakespeare to Pope: An Enquiry into the Causes and Phenomena of the Rise of Classical Poetry in England*. Given the nature of the controversy which followed its publication, the title and the fact that it was published by Cambridge University Press are important.

[49] R. M. Seiler (ed.), *Walter Pater: The Critical Heritage* (London, 1980), 22. For further details of the scandals at Oxford, see Laurel Brake, 'Judas and the Widow', in Philip Dodd (ed.), *Walter Pater: An Imaginative Sense of Fact* (London, 1981), 39–54; Richard Ellmann, *Oscar Wilde* (London, 1987), 58–64; Billie Andrew Inman, 'Estrangement and Connection: Walter Pater, Benjamin Jowett and William M. Hardinge', in Laurel Brake and Ian Small (eds.), *Walter Pater in the 1990s* (Greensboro, NC, forthcoming, 1991).

the alleged hedonism of the book's conclusion. Some critics, however, noticed the inadequacy of the book's scholarship. Specialists, such as Sidney Colvin, Mrs Mark Pattison, and Sarah Wister pointed out its shortcomings as cultural and art history. (It is worth remembering in this respect that Pater changed the title of the book's second edition in 1877 to the less provocative *The Renaissance: Studies in Art and Poetry*.) But such criticism in the main went unnoticed, partly because Pater's critics had bigger fish to fry, but partly, too, because Pater had not set himself up as scholarly authority in the manner of a Jacob Burckhardt or even a John Addington Symonds. This qualification was not lost on contemporary critics: although they noted that Pater made errors in his work, they noted also that the preface stated fairly forcefully that the authority for the type of criticism he was practising resided in the sensibility of the critic, and not in any body of specialist fact or theory.

Although the situation with Edmund Gosse ten years later was in many ways apparently similar, the controversy was of a quite different nature. In 1884, after the resignation of Leslie Stephen, Gosse was appointed as the second Clark lecturer at Trinity College, Cambridge and *From Shakespeare to Pope* was the text of those lectures. The initial reviews, if not enthusiastic, were certainly not critical. But in 1886 John Churton Collins published a long condemnation of Gosse's pretensions to scholarship. Collins was to become professor of English at Birmingham, but at the time he was virtually excluded from the academic establishment, particularly in Oxford. Contemporary and modern accounts have emphasized the personal nature of the consequent scandal, and indeed personal rivalry and the betrayal of friendship were issues.[50] Churton Collins had been a friend of Gosse—a point which Gosse subsequently made a great deal of. Moreover, Gosse had received academic preferment, and Collins had recently failed to win the nomination to the Merton chair of English at Oxford. In addition, there were obvious pathological factors involved, for Collins's papers

---

[50] For the most comprehensive account of the controversy, see Ann Thwaite, *Edmund Gosse: A Literary Landscape, 1849–1928* (London, 1984), 277–97; see also Anthony Kearney, *John Churton Collins: The Louse on the Locks of Literature* (Edinburgh, 1986), 52–69.

reveal that he had a deeply depressive personality.[51] Moreover, the episode with Gosse was part of Collins's long campaign to change the nature of English studies at English universities.[52] But these features, even taken collectively, do not explain why the controversy should have taken on such a public dimension. In fact there is another element to the dispute which has tended to be overlooked. Collins's review was a damning list of the scholarly and historical errors to be found in Gosse's book: the work was a tissue of half-facts and half-truths. The nub of Collins's case was that Gosse's claims to possess a critical and scholarly authority turned out on inspection to be counterfeit. Early in his review Collins commented, '[t]hat such a book as this should have been permitted to go forth to the world with the *imprimatur* of the University of Cambridge, affords matter for very grave reflection'. After a long list of Gosse's errors, he noted, 'And this is a University Lecturer!'[53] Collins's point was at heart one about authority. Contemporary literary history, conducted under the aegis of universities, ought, Collins maintained, to be sustained by the accepted standards of scholarly research, of which verifiability of evidence was perhaps the most important. Literary scholarship ought in the first place, that is, to submit itself to the kind of factual scrutiny which was becoming commonplace in the social sciences and in history.

However, it is the reaction of Gosse's associates and intimates, drawn principally from London literati, which is of real interest. Henry James and Thomas Hardy, for example, wrote to Gosse to assure him that it was Collins who had appeared vituperative. Both read the review as a straightforward personal attack—for Hardy, Collins was simply 'in a rage' and James wrote that Gosse had been 'ponderously and maliciously attacked by an old friend'.[54] When Gosse replied to Collins's criticism in the pages of the *Athenaeum* a little later, James wrote

[51] Churton Collins's notebooks at Birmingham University (MS. BUL 4/V) reveal quite graphically his long periods of depression and despair.

[52] Some of the larger issues of Collins's career are addressed by Tony Pinkney, 'Lice and Literature: On Churton Collins', *News from Nowhere* 3 (1987), 34–9. See also Phyllis Grosskurth, 'Churton Collins: Scourge of the Late Victorians', *University of Toronto Quarterly*, 34 (1965), 254–68; and Evan Charteris, *Life and Letters of Sir Edmund Gosse* (London, 1931), 193–9.

[53] John Churton Collins, 'English Literature at the Universities', *Quarterly Review*, 163 (1886), 289, 301.

[54] See Thwaite, *Edmund Gosse*, 288, 290.

to him with the assurance that he had vindicated himself; and Pater felt that Gosse had 'lightly, gracefully, promptly, over-turned' his 'ponderous antagonist'.[55] Other figures who responded in broadly the same terms included Tennyson, Swinburne, William Archer, Robert Buchanan, and Richard Garnett. Gosse's distinguished literary friends chose to see the controversy in simple personal terms, in which he was the wronged party and had endured a malicious and ungentle-manly attack. Other contributors to the debate which ensued saw the larger issues, particularly that of the importance of scholar-ship. Gosse's friends tried to claim for him the authority which Pater had invoked in *The Renaissance*—that of the critic, for whom authority resided still in individual prestige, rather than that of the scholar for whom authority resided in the collective judgement of the academic community. Hence, in the opinions of Gosse's friends, there was a contrast, but no real conflict, between critical sensibility and scholarly accuracy. They mer-ely invoked different sorts of authority for themselves. The authority of the critic resided in the nature of his reactions, or in the quality of his judgements and his sensibilities—finally in simply who he was. Factual accuracy, the domain of the scholar, could neither confirm nor refute such judgements. A similar contrast between scholarship and critical judgement had of course existed in reactions to *The Renaissance* a decade earlier, but the opposition between scholarship and criticism had not been popularly perceived in terms of a crisis. The crisis occurred simply because the nature of criticism, and the grounds upon which it might be conducted, had changed in the intervening decade. And it is worth noting that the divergence between critical judgement (dependent exclusively upon sens-ibility, and deriving authority solely from that), and other forms of literary critical discourse (the authority of which is dependent upon the approbation of a scholarly community or an academic institution) has formed the basis of profound disagreements in the study of literature in the century since Collins's review. Beneath the disagreement are opposing views about the significance of history and historical research in

---

[55] Gosse's letter was published in the *Athenaeum* on 23 Oct. 1886, pp. 534–5; for Pater's comments, see *Letters of Walter Pater*, ed. Lawrence Evans (Oxford, 1970), 67. Pater's letter was dated 24 Oct. 1886.

criticism, and opposing views about the nature of criticism itself.

APPENDIX

Economic historians have isolated four main issues in their accounts of the marginal revolution. These are: (1) Whether the marginal revolution was in fact a revolution or simply an aspect of a lengthy process of change in economic thought in Europe. (2) The nature of change within social science—how far, that is, changes within economics were theoretical developments produced within the discipline and how far they were responses to larger political and social factors. (3) Whether the multiple discovery of the theory of marginal utility (by William Stanley Jevons in Britain, Léon Walras in Switzerland, and Carl Menger in Austria) was in fact a true 'multiple'. (4) To what extent the theories of economics produced at the time caused the academic and institutionalized specialization and professionalization of the subject. For discussion of these issues, see the following accounts, from which my knowledge of marginalism is derived: Paul Adelman, 'Frederic Harrison and the "Positivist" Attack on Orthodox Political Economy', *History of Political Economy*, 3 (1971), 170–89; R. D. Collison Black, 'W. S. Jevons and the Foundation of Modern Economics', *History of Political Economy*, 4 (1972), 364–78; S. G. Checkland, 'Economic Opinion in England as Jevons found It', *Manchester School*, 2 (1951), 143–69; A. W. Coats, 'Sociological Aspects of British Economic Thought (ca. 1880–1930)', *Journal of Political Economy*, 75 (1967), 706–27; id., 'Role of Authority in the Development of British Economics', *Journal of Law and Economics*, 7 (1964), 85–106; id., 'Economic and Social Context of the Marginal Revolution of the 1870's', in R. D. Collison Black, A. W. Coats, Craufurd D. W. Goodwin (eds.), *Marginal Revolution in Economics: Interpretation and Evaluation* (Durham, NC, 1973), 37–58; R. D. Collison Black, 'Papers and Correspondence of William Stanley Jevons: A Supplementary Note', *Manchester School*, 50 (1982), 417–28; Mark Blaug, 'Was there a Marginal Revolution?', in Black, Coats, Goodwin (eds.), *Marginal Revolution in Economics*, 3–14; N. B. deMarchi, 'Noxious Influence of Authority: A Correction of Jevons's Charge', *Journal of Law and Economics*, 16 (1973), 179–89; Robert B. Ekelund, jun., and Robert F. Hébert, *History of Economic Theory and Method* (1975; 2nd edn., New York, 1983); Robert M. Fisher, *Logic of Economic Discovery: Neoclassical Economics and the Marginal Revolution* (Brighton, 1986); T. W. Hutchison, *Review of Economic Doctrines 1870–1929* (Westport, Conn. 1975); id., *On Revolutions and Progress in Economic Knowledge*

(Cambridge, 1978); id., 'Politics and Philosophy in Jevons's Political Economy', *Manchester School*, 50 (1982), 366–78; John Maynard Keynes, 'William Stanley Jevons 1835–1882: A Centenary Allocution on his Life as Economist and Statistician', *Journal of the Royal Statistical Society*, 99 (1936), 516–48; Gerard M. Koot, 'English Historical Economics and the Emergence of Economic History in England', *History of Political Economy*, 12 (1980), 174–205; David Laidler, 'Jevons on Money', *Manchester School*, 50 (1982), 326–53; John Maloney, *Marshall: Orthodoxy and the Professionalisation of Economics* (Cambridge, 1985); Joseph V. Remenyi, 'Core Demi-Core Interaction: Toward a General Theory of Disciplinary and Subdisciplinary Growth', *History of Political Economy*, 11 (1979), 30–63; Lionel Robbins, 'Place of Jevons in the History of Economic Thought', *Manchester School*, 50 (1982), 310–25; Warren J. Samuels, 'History of Economic Thought as Intellectual History', *History of Political Economy*, 6 (1974), 305–23; Stephen M. Stigler, 'Jevons as Statistician', *Manchester School*, 50 (1982), 354–65.

3

Aesthetics, Psychology, and Biology

I have argued in the previous chapter that common to the history of political economy, historiography, and sociology in the middle years of the nineteenth century was a debate about, and changes in, the epistemological assumptions used to underwrite their intellectual authority. And these changes in their turn coincided with (and indeed helped to enable) these same disciplines to be accommodated within the general process of professionalization and institutionalization outlined in my Introduction. Moreover, these two processes ensured the virtual marginalization of the non-professional intellectual, and thus of what Oscar Wilde later called 'Individualism'. One newly defined and recently professionalized discipline of knowledge, however, seemed in all its epistemological assumptions to endorse at an abstract level the whole notion of individualism. That discipline was psychology. Psychology defined its object of study, the mind, in terms of individual perceptions, impressions, and desires. Such a paradigm was of precisely the kind which would attract those working without institutional endorsement or those marginalized within particular institutions.

It is practically a tautology to say that at any historical moment a constant, if not necessarily direct, relationship will exist between the way in which literary and art criticism is practised and the dominant assumptions in aesthetics, simply because one way of conceiving of the discipline of aesthetics is as the elaboration of the theoretical presuppositions which make a critical discourse possible. It is to be expected, then, that in the last decades of the nineteenth century the lack of general agreement about the nature of literary and art criticism should be accompanied by an equal sense of disquiet in aesthetic speculation. There was a wide-ranging debate at the time about the nature of the aesthetic, and a strong body of opinion held to the view that aesthetic response could finally be described in terms of affective states. One of the main issues in this debate was the nature of the relationship which aesthetics as a discipline was thought to have with other disciplines of knowledge; the most important of these was its relationship with the new 'science' of psychology.

In 1886 James Ward, the Cambridge psychologist, contributed to the ninth edition of the *Encyclopaedia Britannica* its entry on psychology.[1] For an essay in an encyclopedia it proved to be remarkably controversial. It provoked a review by Alexander Bain, perhaps the most eminent British psychologist of the time, in *Mind*, the periodical which Bain had himself founded a decade earlier, and at that time still the most influential academic journal in Britain. The lively debate which ensued in the pages of *Mind* lasted throughout the following year.[2] What Ward had in effect done was to throw down a challenge to a powerful orthodoxy in British psychology. As matters turned out, that challenge proved to be successful, for within a few years it led to the abandoning of two fundamental principles which had distinguished British psychology for at least thirty years and which had been the reason for Bain's rise to eminence. Both principles embodied a form of nineteenth-century scientific reductionism, but were by the early 1880s commonplaces in psychology. The first was that association was the basic characteristic of all conscious and unconscious mental functioning. The second was the principle that all mental mechanisms which psychology had investigated were themselves finally to be explained in terms of physiological processes. Generally it had been the tendency of psychological theory in Britain for the preceding thirty years or so to locate psychology as a discipline firmly in the realm of the natural sciences, rather than as an aspect of philosophy, the dominant view during the eighteenth century and early part of the nineteenth. Contemporary research into localized nerve sensations and into localized brain functions had permitted the postulation of a series of theoretical relationships between

[1] James Ward, 'Psychology', *Encyclopaedia Britannica* (9th edn., Edinburgh, 1875–1901), xx. 66–75.

[2] Alexander Bain, 'Mr James Ward's "Psychology"', *Mind*, 11 (1886), 457–77. See also id., 'On "Association" Controversies', *Mind*, 12 (1887), 161–82; James Ward, 'Psychological Principles (III)', *Mind*, 12 (1887), 45–67; Alexander Bain, 'On Mr Ward's "Psychological Principles"', *Mind*, 12 (1887), 311–13.

psychology and neurology, itself 'new' in the sense that it had only recently been established in relation to other areas of physiology. The consequence was that psychology as a discipline of knowledge in the middle of the nineteenth century had been redefined. Following this redefinition, psychology shared a number of concepts and terms with the discipline of physiology. Adjacent to psychology also—and inevitably so—was the recently revolutionized discipline of biology. The most distinguished figures among those who wanted to connect absolutely the domains of psychology and biology were Charles Darwin and Herbert Spencer. For both men it was axiomatic that psychology as a discipline of knowledge could be theoretically justified only by incorporating into it the methodologies of the natural sciences. And consequently what formed the practical centre of that domain of knowledge was the scientific (or allegedly scientific) study of affects. Psychology in the hands of Darwin, Bain, and Spencer, the main voices in the orthodoxy which Ward criticized, became what may be called an *affective psychology*.

James Ward's challenge in 1886 was an attempt to restore the concept of the subject to the centre of psychological enquiry. Both associational and physiological psychology had maintained the fragmentary nature of sensation and ultimately—as will become clear—the fragmentary nature of perception, too. In Bain's and Spencer's terms, perception could be reduced to absolutely discrete 'units'—to differentiated impressions which were fundamentally affective in character. Ward opposed this view. It was his thesis that all mental life could best be described by postulating an active agency which was capable of either assimilating, rejecting, or ranking sensations and perceptions. It was this agency—rather than the simple and uncontrolled accumulation of impressions—which, according to Ward, formed consciousness. As a result of Ward's challenge, British psychology became less exclusively concerned with affective states.

For the historian of British aesthetics, however, there is an interesting consequence to the way in which associational and physiological psychology specified its object of study during the middle years of the nineteenth century. The experimental science which Bain, Darwin, and Spencer defined in terms of its adjacency to biology and physiology had also established a community of terms and concepts with another and much more unlikely discipline, itself only recently invented: that of formal aesthetics. (Or perhaps, for reasons which I describe below, it would be more accurate to say that the philosophy of art and aesthetics reasserted the community of its object of study with that of the discipline of psychology.)

It is fairly widely accepted that the study of aesthetics (in the sense that the term is now understood) was of eighteenth-century origin, and that it was Kant who finally established the aesthetic as an autonomous category in philosophic thought. The term 'aesthetic' was used initially to designate sense-perception: to define how objects became perceptible to, or apprehended by, the senses. As historians of philosophy in the 1880s frequently pointed out, it was the German philosopher Alexander Baumgarten who appropriated the term 'aesthetic' in his work *Aesthetica* (1750–8) and began to change its use. Baumgarten limited its reference to denote above all the science or philosophy of taste rather than of mere feeling; and so, by implication, he anticipated its consequent restriction to denote only the science or philosophy of the beautiful.[3] In this limited sense, the term had gained currency in Germany steadily but slowly; in Britain, the first restricted usage (that is, in Baumgarten's sense) occurred only in the late 1830s. However, the term 'aesthetics' used to designate sense-perception alone was of an older vintage: in fact its first usage occurs very early in the nineteenth century. (Indeed in 1879 George Henry Lewes, in his role as a popularizer of science and psychology, tried to coin a word which would include this idea of a science of feeling —'aesthesics'.[4] Only by the 1850s did the term 'aesthetics' find general acceptance as a description of a legitimate and self-justifying discipline of knowledge. Of course what we now recognize and label as aesthetic enquiry had in fact taken place, but under the aegis of different disciplines of thought; indeed, prior to this time, aesthetic and moral beauty were categories which tended not to be properly distinguished from each other.

[3] See Alexander Baumgarten, *Aesthetica* (Frankfurt-on-Oder, 1750–8). Baumgarten claims that aesthetics is the science of sensory perception ('scientia cognitionis sensitivae'.)

[4] See G. H. Lewes, *Study of Psychology* (London, 1879). One of Lewes's main concerns in the book was to examine how psychology constitutes its object of study in contrast to that of physiology.

What happened when psychologists tried to describe aesthetic responses in terms of psychology during the last decades of the nineteenth century, therefore, was only an attempt to revive the older meaning of the term 'aesthetic', to relocate and redescribe it, as it were, more precisely in the realm of the most appropriate scientific study of the conditions of sensory perception, that of physiological psychology.

The result of this relocation of aesthetics was far-reaching. Theoretical speculation began to come to terms with how aesthetic response could be described and predicted scientifically, in both associational and physiological terms. The argument ran along the following lines. If the term 'aesthetic' referred to a mode of perception, or to a distinct kind of experience initially made possible by a mode of perception, then it followed that aesthetics was amenable to psychological investigations; and, moreover, if the two discourses were contiguous, and their respective practices related, then it also followed that the methods and procedures of Bain's and Spencer's new scientific psychology could be applied to an investigation of aesthetic responses. In other words, responses to art would produce physiological and psychological affects fundamentally no different from all the other affective states which psychology had attempted to investigate. (Inevitably, as I shall try to point out below, the problems involved in defining the ways in which art-objects were marked off from other objects were never addressed. Such a qualification was of course a debilitating handicap in any attempt to produce a theory of *art*, but it was an inescapable consequence of attempting to redefine a theory of art in terms of a theory of aesthetic perception alone.) In the arguments of psychologists, it followed that the experience of art could be reduced to a series of discrete, although related, affects which derived from predictable physiological conditions and which had predictable physiological consequences.

As matters turned out, none of the major psychologists involved attempted any such investigation in the detail which would have been necessary for a psychology of aesthetics to be convincing; indeed, it is extremely difficult to envisage how such a project might have been successfully conducted then (or indeed at any other time). But none the less all the major British theorists of psychology, including Darwin and Spencer, examined the concept of the aesthetic and the range of possible aesthetic experience, and included discussions of them in their general theories of human behaviour. Indeed, their reluctance to embark upon a detailed project seems to have been based solely on a sense of priorities. So, for example, Herbert Spencer in his *Principles of Psychology* declined to describe a full psychology of aesthetics, not through any misgivings about the procedural or theoretical difficulties which might have been encountered, but simply for reasons of space.[5] That aesthetic response could be investigated scientifically, and that its effects could therefore be predicted with scientific precision, was a view never seriously doubted until the last years of the century.

Given the nature of modern scientific publications, what now appears to us to be an esoteric and particularly specialized branch of scientific knowledge was, in Victorian Britain, conducted in a very open manner. Certainly the principal figures concerned in the construction of a scientifically based aesthetics were familiar and famous names in the field of nineteenth-century science and intellectual life. The original speculative work of men such as Bain, Spencer, and Darwin was disseminated by a group of popularizing writers of whom James Sully and Grant Allen are perhaps the best known. In addition, the debate about the psychology of aesthetics, like many Victorian scientific controversies, was very public. Spencer's *Principles* went into a second edition in 1872 and in 1881 a revised third edition of the work had a printing of over four thousand. Alexander Bain began work slightly before Spencer, and continued long after the latter's death. He enjoyed less general prestige but was an even more influential figure among specialists. Indeed, Bain's work remained the standard textbooks for the teaching of psychology for at least fifty years.[6] However, the most significant testimony to the wide public interest in the new

[5] See Herbert Spencer, *Principles of Psychology* (2 vols., 1855; 3rd edn., London, 1881), esp. vol. ii, *passim*.

[6] An interesting anecdote about Bain's work was related to me by the late Geoffrey Shepherd: his father, who had trained as a teacher early in this century, had been recommended to read Bain as a standard psychological textbook long after his work had been superseded. For more verifiable evidence, see *Brett's History of Psychology*, ed. R. S. Peters (London, 1953) and D. B. Klein, *History of Scientific Psychology* (London, 1970).

science of psychology and in speculation about a full-blown science of aesthetics exists in the fact that the main forums for the debate were the leading Victorian periodicals—the *Westminster Review*, the *Contemporary Review*, and, principally, the *Fortnightly Review*—publications which have no present-day equivalents.

Now in order to survey the general features of this debate, it is convenient, although not chronologically precise, to use the work of Herbert Spencer as a point of departure. In his *Principles of Psychology* Spencer attempted to develop some ideas which he had first encountered in the fifteenth of Friedrich Schiller's *Letters on the Aesthetic Education of Man*. Basically he was concerned with exploring the relationship between art and pleasure.[7] Spencer distinguished between what he considered to be two fundamentally opposed kinds of human activity: the widest category was that containing those actions which, physically serving the ends of the organism, were held to be life-enhancing or life-sustaining. Most human actions, in Spencer's view, naturally fell into this category. Spencer's other category contained actions which had no ends other than their own execution, because they provided no immediate physical benefit to the organism. It was in this latter category that Spencer located both physiologically and psychologically (for, as I have noted, there was to be no final distinction between the two disciplines) what he called 'man's proto-aesthetic' impulses. These represented human 'play-impulses'. Generically in Spencer's scheme, artistic and aesthetic pleasures belonged to that type of activity which was undertaken for its own sake: indeed they epitomized the type. The more superfluous an action to the basic biological needs of an organism (which in fact was Spencer's rather inaccurate account of Schiller's 'play-impulse'—*spieltrieb*)[8] the more pleasure it had necessarily to

---

[7] It is interesting to note in passing that perhaps the most influential and certainly the best-known psychological investigation into aesthetic experience, that of Freud, also emphasizes the pleasurable aspects of art in order to account for its popularity.

[8] See Friedrich Schiller, *On the Aesthetic Education of Man*, tr. Elizabeth M. Wilkinson and L. A. Willoughby (Oxford, 1967), 101–9. Schiller in fact gives considerably more weight to the notion of play than Spencer allows: 'man only plays when he is in the fullest sense of the word a human being, and he is only fully a human being when he plays' (p. 107). The relationship between play and the aesthetic had recently been discussed by Alexander Bain in *Mental and Moral Science* (London, 1868–72), and by J. F. Seeley in 'Elementary Principles in Art', *Macmillan's Magazine* 16 (1867), 1–12.

yield, simply to be valuable to the organism in question. This was Spencer's central concept. An experience (and in terms of art, Spencer did not distinguish between creating a work of art and responding to one) was aesthetic if it could be said to possess no ulterior purpose other than its own execution—if it was, physiologically speaking, superfluous; if it existed, that is, simply for its own sake and for no other end. And moreover, the *quality* of that experience was determined solely by the *quantity* or yield of pleasure which the experience was capable of providing for the individual concerned. The greatest art therefore axiomatically became that which was capable of exercising the greatest variety and volume of pleasurable emotion or sensation in its audience.

What Spencer had done was to produce an account of aesthetic experience which was fundamentally affective in character, and from that account of aesthetic experience he produced a definition of art. The features or attributes of a work of art, if they were of any significance at all, were only secondary, because the art-object itself entered his argument only as the cause of a sensation or an emotional condition in the spectator, listener, or reader. An attribute or feature of a work of art for Spencer was only a kind of stimulus which would produce a predictable sensation or bring about a uniform and familiar emotional response. Of course, Spencer was most at ease when discussing the range of emotional effects produced by, say, particular colours or particular musical chords or tones.[9] These particular examples clearly lent themselves best to a demonstration of a typology of musical affects.

For the sake of clarity it ought perhaps to be noted at this point that it is difficult to see any lasting value in what Spencer was attempting. It is a widely held view among most philosophers of art that a work of art can produce a varied and on occasions inconsistent range of emotional responses in the spectator, listener, or reader. The only criteria for assessing the appropriateness or otherwise of responses to a particular work lie not in a theory of aesthetic response but in a theory of art.

Philosophical considerations of the relationship between the aesthetic and pleasure persisted until the 1890s; see Henry Rutgers Marshall, 'Hedonic Aesthetics', *Mind*, NS 2 (1893), 15–41; id., *Pain, Pleasure and Aesthetics* (London, 1894).

[9] See Spencer, *Principles of Psychology*, 627–48.

However, this is a qualification which, although true of Spencer's account of aesthetics, applies equally to all attempts to construct a psychology of aesthetics.

The lines of enquiry which Spencer had indicated in general terms were taken up most fruitfully by James Sully. Sully was a prolific and cogent writer who quickly achieved popularity and some eminence in scientific and philosophical circles. He wrote frequently for most of the major periodicals and was a regular contributor to the early numbers of *Mind* (which, in its first years and under Alexander Bain's guidance, had a pronounced bias towards publishing work on psychological research). Sully's ideas about the fundamental relationship between aesthetics and psychology were developed during the 1880s and they are perhaps best approached via his polemical essay 'Art and Psychology' which appeared in the first volume of *Mind* in 1876. But in fact his principal arguments had been expounded equally elaborately two years previously in *Sensation and Intuition* (1874) and broached as early as 1871 in an essay entitled 'The Aesthetics of Human Character' in the *Fortnightly Review* which, under the editorship of John Morley, was then considered to be among the more 'advanced' Victorian periodicals.[10] In all these works, Sully's main project was to elaborate upon Darwin's suggestions about the way responses to the perception of form might be explained by reference to evolutionary thinking.

Sully held firmly to the rather naïve proposition that the problems of aesthetics would prove amenable to psychological rather than formal or ontological analysis. He attempted to prove his case by enlarging upon what Spencer had claimed in his *Principles*, namely that it was 'yield of pleasure' which formed the basis of an aesthetic experience or emotion. Indeed, so completely did Sully adhere to Spencer's views that they quickly became axioms in his work and were presented to the reader as formulaic definitions: art provided, quite simply, 'the highest conceivable quality and quantity of human pleasure'.[11] (The consumerist metaphors of pleasure and pain proposed here have interesting similarities with the language of mar-

---

[10] See James Sully, 'Art and Psychology', *Mind*, 1 (1876), 467–78; id., 'Aesthetics of Human Character', *Fortnightly Review*, NS 9 (1871), 505–20; id., *Sensation and Intuition* (London, 1874).

[11] Sully, *Sensation and Intuition*, 349.

ginalism, especially that of Jevons, discussed in Chapter 2; moreover, the formulaic reduction of concepts of beauty to concepts of pleasure has remarkable affinities with the claims for art made by later critics, particularly by those of the Aesthetic Movement.) There were, however, less reductive aspects to Sully's work, for he did considerably more than simply popularize his sources. In fact, he elaborated Spencer's arguments in two quite crucial ways, both of which permitted the accommodation of psychological speculation about aesthetics into the much larger and more general theory of perception which had been developed by British psychologists from the late 1850s onwards. Sully's first main line of argument concluded that pleasure was vouchedsafe to the spectator of art by means of an intervening *impression*. His Victorian readers met this view formulated once again in terms of an axiom:

A work of art, for whatever order of mind it may be specially fitted, must satisfy the general conditions of pleasurable impression. . . . Thus it is a distinguishing mark of artistic activity that it is fitted to afford an immediate delight by the medium of a visible or audible impression.[12]

Sully's second original contribution to the psychology of aesthetics was a consequence of the first. As the means by which art generated pleasure in the mind of the spectator or audience was the sense-impression, and as all impressions were by definition discrete and unique, so Sully maintained that all responses to works of art *had necessarily* to be individual as well. The theoretical postulate of an 'impression' served to confirm the proposition that all responses to art were fundamentally *relative* to the particular audiences in question; it also made anything other than a relative aesthetic difficult to conceive of, or at least very difficult to make consonant with the premises of psychology. And once again Sully presented his point in terms of a slogan or formula, that an 'aesthetic impression presents itself as something eminently inconstant and relative'.[13] According to his essay in *Mind* in 1876, Sully considered that it was only the procedures of psychology which could possibly investigate and describe individual responses to art, relative

12 Ibid. 347, 341.
13 Ibid. 347.

and inconstant as they were. In Sully's view, any attempt to generalize—his term is 'dogmatize'—about aesthetic response was not only misguided, but it was also unhelpful.

Now, as I have indicated, the most significant and debilitating omission from this particular line of reasoning is simply that it concentrates upon the spectator, audience, or reader to the exclusion of all other considerations. Anything other than the mechanisms which control the spectator's mental or emotional responses are, strictly speaking, an irrelevance to a *psychology* of aesthetics. In Sully's case, for instance, it obviated the need to provide any arguments for defining or investigating the concept of art itself. The consequence of this argument was the failure to consider any possible relationships which may exist between a concept of art and a concept of aesthetic response. The object of Spencer's, Sully's, and Bain's 'new' science, as it concerned aesthetics, was the investigation of a response which was the product of a transaction between the spectator and the work under contemplation, and nothing more. The general drift of the thesis, therefore, was to dismiss as irrelevant the *kind* or the *quality* of artefact which produced the particular emotional or mental state under investigation. Although both Spencer and Sully did in fact try to establish a series of correspondences between the type of art experienced and the type of affective states allegedly produced by it—a typology of affects, that is—the logical tendency of their arguments was to diminish considerably the importance of the art-object, or even in some cases to threaten to abolish completely the entire category of art-objects. If aesthetic responses were finally to be assimilated into a larger description or taxonomy of affective states, as both Spencer and Sully had hoped, then not only did the particularity of the artefact become unimportant, but so too ultimately did the whole concept of the art-object, for, by definition, all other artefacts or naturally occurring objects were capable of producing similar, if not so extreme, affective states in the spectator or audience. The real consequence of Spencer's and Sully's work —although naturally it was never stated, nor perhaps even properly realized—was to remove entirely any difference between art and non-art. The only criterion which could possibly be used to distinguish between art and non-art was that art-objects would increase the intensity and frequency of certain mental and emotional states. The corollary of this point, although again it was never stated explicitly, was that it now became logical to suggest that it was the *quality* of certain responses, perceptions, or experiences—their reliability and intensity, for example—which would constitute those experiences as experiences of *art*, art now being defined in terms of what produces a transaction between spectator and object, rather than in terms of qualities or features of the object itself. At this point it is perhaps useful to recall Postlethwaite's aesthetic contemplation of a lily in Du Maurier's cartoon—his contemplation of a naturally occurring object, that is. He is not simply carrying out the injunctions of a Wilde or a Pater to 'experience life in the manner of art'. According to late nineteenth-century psychology, Postlethwaite's reactions are *normal*, in the sense that he is engaging the world by means of an 'aesthetic attitude'. Psychology, that is, had arrived at a theory of aesthetic perception which was strikingly close to that enjoined in the polemic of the Aesthetes.

Despite these implicit but profound theoretical contradictions, the general scheme for a psychology of aesthetics acquired popular advocates. Spencer's and Sully's work was of central importance in establishing a discourse in which *impression, pleasure*, and *the relative* figured as key psychological and key aesthetic terms. This vocabulary—and the concepts which had generated it—became a familiar rhetoric in the hands of non-specialist writers on psychology. Here a popularizer like Grant Allen presents something of a representative case. In his *Physiological Aesthetics* (1877), for example, Allen synthesized the work of many British psychologists in order to establish the propositions that any aesthetic response could be defined in the first place in terms of pleasure, and that the series of 'pleasurable impressions' which formed an aesthetic experience could be further analysed in terms of simple sensory and stimulus response. It was the burden of Allen's argument that aesthetic responses would all finally prove amenable to redescription in purely physiological terms—such as physiological reactions to tones, chords, colours, patterns, and so forth. The whole debate generated a series of concepts and a terminology, which, as my later discussions of Pater and Wilde will make clear, was shared by an entire school of 'impressionist' critics.

Sully's and Allen's conclusions about the nature of perception thus had an element of the commonplace to them, for in their turn they were determined by a general theory of personality generated by other areas of psychology; and so the speculation about psychological aesthetics which took place in Britain in the 1870s and 1880s ought to be placed in the context of the much larger and more general psychological theory from which its assumptions derived.

This general theory was in its turn indebted for its principal theses and most of its detail to the work of Alexander Bain. As I have indicated, Bain was the single most influential figure in nineteenth-century British psychology, more important even than Spencer in determining the general development of the subject. John Stuart Mill went so far as to claim that Bain had 're-introduced' psychology as a serious discipline of knowledge into Britain. Working in the 1850s and the 1860s in Aberdeen, Bain produced three highly influential works, *The Senses and the Intellect* (1855), *The Emotions and the Will* (1859), and *Mental and Moral Science* ((1868–72). One of Bain's main ideas was that the nervous system and the brain comprised an organic unit and thus *any* mental processes could be examined physiologically. Bain also attempted to define consciousness, his most thorough account of the topic occurring in *The Emotions and the Will*. Here Bain asserted that change was the essential pre-condition for consciousness. The fundamental property of the human brain, he maintained, was its ability to discriminate between consecutive sense-impressions. So in Bain's thesis, consciousness became defined as a series of impressions which were differentiated from each other by novelty or by what he called 'surprise'. The greater the difference or discrimination between these impressions, the more 'conscious' the recipient of those impressions necessarily had to be. Such an ability was the basis of all mental activity: 'the brain is more sharply stimulated . . . by reason of the novelty of impression . . . The clear, distinct discrimination that we obtain of different things that strike us . . . is the very foundation of our intellectual development'.[14] Bain argued that it was the nature of the individual mind to

[14] Alexander Bain, *Emotions and the Will* (1859; 2nd edn., London, 1865), 571–2.

dwell upon the uniqueness of an impression, upon those qualities which differentiated one impression from the multitudes
preceding or following it. Cognition, he went on to argue, was
made possible only by the patterns formed by 'associated
impressions'. And it was language above all else which invested
an impression or series of impressions with permanence: for
Bain, that is, the fixing of specific (but selected) impressions
was made possible by the act of naming, and thus permanent
patterns of cognition were formed. In fact Bain's argument at
this point was little more than a refinement of some of the
concepts of Associationism which he had inherited from
psychologists in the early part of the century: they had proposed a very similar account of what makes cognition possible.
For Bain, what distinguished the refined or highly developed
intellect—the civilized mind, that is—was its ability to distinguish between impressions: the higher the level of intellectual
development, the more precisely and subtly it could discriminate between the impressions which it received. It was the
quality of highly discriminated impressions which typified a
human aesthetic response.

By the 1870s, then, psychology had clearly revealed how
close its domain of knowledge lay to that of some literary and
art criticism. Psychology had developed and refined theoretical
concepts which speculation in aesthetics could easily appropriate or use. First it had described aesthetic responses solely in
terms of affects, in which the perception of a work of art was
constituted by an 'impression' or series of 'impressions' of it.
Next it had defined art in terms of the number of *pleasurable
impressions* which it was capable of yielding; further it had
suggested that the means by which the mind received an
impression was conditioned by the fact that impressions were
by their very nature *relative*. Finally it had concluded that the
most civilized mind was the one which could most subtly and
most fully discriminate its impressions. This vocabulary and
the concepts associated with it found their way into the practice
of a number of literary and art critics over the next twenty years
or so. I use the expression 'found their way' because, while it is
clear that the whole area of psychology and psychopathology
interested writers in the 1890s and while it is also clear that
psychopathological terms were used to characterize both artists

and their work,[15] to assert that there were any individual acts of appropriation is reductive, and misrepresents the nature of the intellectual influences at work. Rather it is the case that the practice of contemporary critics indicates a process of gradual realignment in the relationships between bodies of knowledge and the epistemology invoked to validate that knowledge. This process can be illustrated by any number of examples. For brevity, I choose only two, both of which, however, are famous and typical. The first exemplifies the way art and literary criticism took over the vocabulary generated by affective psychology; and the second illustrates the common use that the disciplines of aesthetics and psychology made of the concept of association.

That the impressionist criticism of the Aesthetic Movement absorbed and utilized both the conceptual framework and terminology of psychology is a case that can best be sustained by a close analysis of contemporary critical works. The terms 'relative', 'impression', 'discrimination', and 'pleasure' echo through critical writing in the years between 1870 and 1895. The term *impression*, for example, constantly figures as a key lexical item in the critical writing of Swinburne, Pater, and Wilde. The modern reader is often not precisely sure of its contemporary significance but is always aware of the fact that the term is a special one. One famous example will demonstrate the power of this 'loaded' vocabulary. In the preface to *The Renaissance* Pater proposed the first of his famous accounts of the way works of art are experienced. The terms which had been marked off in physiological and psychological aesthetics form a constant lexical set in the text, and the key concepts of psychology are also frequently present. Pater's argument runs along the following lines: a response to a work of art is constituted in the first place by an *impression* of the contemplated book, picture, or statue. This impression is *relative* to the spectator, and his impressions resolve themselves into pleasurable *moments* and ultimately into *pleasurable sensations*. The ability to dis-

---

[15] The most frequently cited work in this respect is that of sociologists and psychologists such as Max Nordau, Paul Bourget, and Havelock Ellis, all of whom tried to characterize literature and art in terms of the psychopathology of the writers or artists concerned.

criminate his impressions fully and finely in the end defines the successful critic. A representative passage, partly quoted before, is this:

> The aesthetic critic, then, regards all the objects with which he has to do, all works of art, and the fairer forms of nature and human life, as powers or forces producing pleasurable sensations, each of a more or less peculiar and unique kind. This influence he feels, and wishes to explain, analysing it, and reducing it to its elements. To him, the picture, the landscape, the engaging personality in life or in a book . . . are valuable . . . for the property each has of affecting one with a special, unique impression of pleasure.[16]

This passage clearly embodies the intellectual ambitions of nineteenth-century science; but in particular it expresses those ambitions via the concepts and the language of British psychological science in general currency in the years immediately prior to the book's publication. Most importantly for Pater, the experience of art is described in terms of affective aesthetic response: in the words of another famous part of the preface, once more already partly quoted: 'What effect does it produce on me? . . . How is my nature modified by its presence and under its influence?' The language and the conceptual set which made it possible reverberated through critical writing of the next two decades; famously in the work of Oscar Wilde and Henry James, less famously in the work of a whole school of critics such as William Sharp and Lionel Johnson.

My second example concerns the history of the concept of Associationism in the nineteenth century. Associationism was perhaps the greatest legacy of eighteenth-century philosophy to nineteenth-century psychology. It was David Hartley who gave the theory its most systematic and influential form. (Indeed it is he who is credited with first seeing the possibility of a physiological psychology.) Certainly it was Hartley who established the idea that association might be one of the most basic of mental mechanisms. It is an interesting testimony to the attractiveness of the theory of Associationism that the most exhaustive exegesis of it was published in the first part of the nineteenth century—James Mill's *Analysis of the Phenomena of the Human*

---

[16] Pater, *The Renaissance*, ed. Hill, xx.

Mind, a work which first appeared in 1829.[17] Mill argued that ideas are no more than aggregations of feelings, and therefore that consciousness too is constituted by feelings or sensations. Moreover, language (in particular the process of naming) was basically a series of marks for a group of associated sensations or copies of sensations (that is, in the theory of Associationism, for a group of *imagined* objects, for within the theory mental events generally were copies of the sensations produced by real events). Mill was the last thoroughgoing Associationist in the sense that no psychologist in later years sought to explain the totality of mental activities exclusively in terms of associations. Although the use made of Associationism was less ambitious and employed a weaker form of the theory, it is easy to see how some of Mill's principles informed theories of consciousness, such as Bain's, formulated later in the century. In practice this weaker form of the theory of Associationism was used to explore the manner in which higher and more complex mental processes might be attributed to, and so be explained in terms of, simpler and more fundamental *neural* processes. Hence the weaker form of the theory was of considerable explanatory value to physiological psychology, for a physiological account of mental functions, which was then one of the main ambitions of all physiology of the brain, could attempt to identify the neural processes responsible for the mental phenomena which Associationism had described. (Some principle of association, although a much weaker one still, operates within Freudian theory, but with the important provision that Freud's emphasis is upon the mechanisms that inhibit the faculty's operation —mechanisms such as displacement, transference, and so forth.)

While Associationism survived, and in its modified form even prospered, in nineteenth-century psychology, in another of its applications, that of aesthetics, its history was rather more chequered. Associationism, as it is applied to aesthetics, typically maintains that the perception or experience of an object as beautiful is dependent upon, and has its origins in, the associations which the object suggests to the experiencing mind. The

---

[17] See David Hartley, *Observations on Man, his Frame, his Duty and his Expectations* (London, 1749); James Mill, *Analysis of the Phenomena of the Human Mind* (2 vols., London, 1829).

theory had received its most cogent and influential formulation in terms of its aesthetic applications in the work of Archibald Alison, whose *Essays on the Nature and Principles of Taste* (1790) had by the turn of the nineteenth century achieved a fairly widespread philosophical respectability in Britain.[18] But as a theory of aesthetic response Associationism steadily lost prestige during the course of the century, so much so that by the 1890s historians of philosophy were making quite scathing reference to it. For example, the most elaborate survey then available, Bernard Bosanquet's *History of Aesthetic* (1892), seldom mentions Alison's name and discusses Associationism only in the context of Gustav Fechner's work or as a negative influence upon John Ruskin.[19] Moreover, according to William Knight's *The Philosophy of the Beautiful* (1891), Alison's arguments were 'irrelevant' to the problems of aesthetics, and Associationism was the 'degenerate teaching of the *soi-disant* Edinburgh school of Alison and Jeffrey'.[20] The most persuasive, eloquent, and certainly the most influential condemnation of Associationism was Ruskin's in *Modern Painters*. Ruskin distinguished between two sorts of association, neither of which, in his view, accounted properly for the experience of art. The first was 'rational' association, which was the 'interest which an object may bear historically', a phenomenon not properly within the scope of Associationism. The second was 'accidental' association, an involuntary process involving the 'connection of ideas and memories with material things, owing to which those material things are regarded as agreeable'.[21] Quite clearly it was this last category of mental phenomena which Associationism had hoped to account for, but Ruskin dismissed both sorts of association as attempts to deny the objective existence of beauty, and so, as most recent critics of Ruskin have pointed out, tended to constitute an aesthetic theory which bore no necessary relationship to the ethical or

---

[18] See Archibald Alison, *Essays on the Nature and Principles of Taste* (Edinburgh, 1790).

[19] Bernard Bosanquet, *A History of Aesthetic* (London, 1892), 384, 441.

[20] William Knight, *The Philosophy of the Beautiful* (London, 1891), i. 188, 232; ii. 39–45.

[21] Ruskin's account of association occurs in *Modern Painters*. See *Library Edition of the Works of John Ruskin*, ed. E. T. Cook and Alexander Wedderburn (London, 1903), ii. 71–2, 229–47.

religious systems of thought which Ruskin valued so highly.[22]

Most of the unfavourable reactions to Associationism later in the century, however, were not along the lines discussed by Ruskin; rather they were made under the argument that it said nothing about the work of art considered either as work or as art: Associationism failed to account for the object's existence as an *art*-object, which necessarily differed ontologically from other sorts of object. In other words, the objection was that Associationism failed to account for the expressionist or representational aspects of art—objections which, as I have suggested, were also made about the notion of an 'aesthetic attitude'. But to critics whose main interest was not in the art-object, but in the idea of aesthetic experience, this objection was a minor one and perhaps even an irrelevance. Indeed its emphasis upon perception and cognition in a potential audience rather than upon the artefactuality of the object was precisely the virtue and attraction of Associationism. Its insistence upon affective states in the mind of the spectator, reader, or audience, its 'impressive' rather than its 'expressive' qualities, to use Oscar Wilde's succinct formula from *Intentions*, was exactly what made the whole theory attractive.

In an early collection of essays on aesthetics and art criticism entitled *Juvenilia* (1887), the young Vernon Lee saw the possibilities which Associationism offered to critics interested mainly in affective states produced by works of art and in the idea of aesthetic response. Indeed, she went so far as to claim that association explained the psychological processes underlying both the creation of a work of art and its perception by an audience. Early in her essay, she marshalled all the contemporary arguments against Associationism both as an account of mental activity generally and as an aesthetic theory. She claimed that association was the 'pushing aside, in short, of reality to make room for the fictions of imagination or memory'.[23] Moreover, Associationism as an aesthetic theory, she went on, denied the possibility of perceiving the 'reality' of

---

[22] This point has been made by George P. Landow, *Aesthetic and Critical Theories of John Ruskin* (Princeton, NJ, 1971), 104.

[23] Vernon Lee, 'Lake of Charlemagne: An Apology of Association', *Juvenilia* (London, 1887), i. 45.

the artefact: that 'reality', Vernon Lee claimed, tended to become submerged under the plethora of associations which the object wakened in the mind of the spectator. In fact, at this point in her argument, Vernon Lee was doing little more than rehearsing objections made familiar by Ruskin: that association involved non-rational, even unconscious, mental processes, and so by making a 'fictional' re-creation of the object, it 'marred' any objective critical response. But after Vernon Lee had listed most of the standard objections to the theory, she went on to suggest that Associationism described very precisely the way in which responses to art-objects in fact took place. And the term 'fiction'—in the senses that the audience or spectator was engaged in the kind of activity which Roman Ingarden has called 'co-creative'—expressed precisely the appeal of the theory. Vernon Lee argued that association was the essential mental process underlying both artistic creation and aesthetic experience: in so doing she suggested that it described exactly how the mind functioned. Indeed, in discussing how responses to art might be generally characterized, she invoked Associationism as a general psychological theory rather than an exclusively aesthetic one. And, in keeping with the general propositions of physiological psychology, she appealed to evidence derived from evolutionary theory.[24] Evolutionists agreed that aesthetic responses originated in certain explicable biological preferences, so that, for example, the form of a healthy man or woman was, for sound and predictable biological reasons which had been made clear by the principles of natural selection, more pleasing than that of a deformed one. Of course, by the mid-1880s the idea that aesthetic responses were conditioned by biological circumstance, and subject to the same kinds of evolutionary pressure as human physical development had become something of a commonplace. As I have suggested, the proposition that the beautiful, as far as the 'typical' human form was concerned, was the physiologically 'correct' and healthy could trace its pedigree through Herbert Spencer to Darwin. The most recent reiteration of the evolutionists' case had been made by Grant Allen in an essay entitled 'Aesthetic

---

[24] In fact the evolutionary justification for Associationism dates in the first instance from Alison's essays. His and Jeffery's work had been reprinted as recently as 1879.

Evolution in Man' in *Mind* in 1880, where he surveyed contemporary accounts of the alleged evolution of human aesthetic sensibilities. Allen had argued that aesthetic choices have specific physiological origins and that the interest shown by lower animals in the forms, colours, and shapes which act as a stimulus for sexual response were in reality 'proto-aesthetic' feelings. The biological origins of aesthetic feelings, in Allen's view, involved the 'appreciation of the pure and healthy typical specific form'; and, having such a determined origin, the form of the beautiful 'for every kind must similarly be . . . the healthy, the normal, the strong, the perfect.'[25]

Even if Vernon Lee was ignorant of this particular work, her essay certainly indicates a familiarity with the kind of case which Allen was putting forward. In fact, there is a sense at the end of her essay that her real interest is in the study of perception, its psychology, and its applications to aesthetics, for her account of association describes what may best be called a sort of race memory, unconscious in its modes of operation, whereby certain instinctual preferences, necessary for the mechanisms of natural selection, manifest themselves at the level of conscious choice. In her view, association applied in this manner actually worked for a general racial or cultural consensus in aesthetic choices, because it proposed the possibility of a genetically common source for all aesthetic judgements (and so incidentally overcame one of the main objections to Associationism made by Ruskin, namely that aesthetic responses originating in associations were invariably and irredeemably idiosyncratic in their nature). Thus once Associationism was presented within the terms of two of the most powerful contemporary scientific orthodoxies, biology and psychology, rather than in the discredited terms of eighteenth-century empirical philosophy, it became a much more useful explanatory tool for the critic.

Predictably, perhaps, Vernon Lee dismissed the usual objections to Associationism—its inability, as I have suggested, to say anything about art rather than about aesthetic experience —because her main interest was in the psychological theory which made her propositions about aesthetics possible. Her

---

[25] Grant Allen, 'Aesthetic Evolution in Man', *Mind*, 5 (1880), 449.

basic claim was that the mind cannot know the unfamiliar without recourse to the familiar to orient it: the mind, that is, constantly refers the new to the known. Of course this was precisely the pattern of mental behaviour which Association-ism had proposed: 'Do you think that we perceive, much less remember, the totally unknown? Not a bit of it; we merely constantly recognize the already familiar'.[26] Vernon Lee went on to argue that association was involved not only in the processes of perception and cognition, but also in those of creation: impressions, brought together under the power of the faculty of association, were the means by which the 'idea' of a new work of art was formed. Here, too, Vernon Lee was being far from original. The tradition of thought which I have outlined acted as a veritable scientific orthodoxy to confirm her views; and, indeed, once again Grant Allen had put forward a virtually identical case. In *Physiological Aesthetics* he had argued that the process of association was the fundamental human mental activity and consequently that cognition was in essence nothing more than 're-cognition'.[27] Even James Ward in his controversial essay on psychology in the *Encyclopaedia Britannica* had insisted that association was the most important practical principle in aesthetic response.[28]

Vernon Lee's belief in the power of an object or a landscape to evoke overwhelming memories and associated images per-sisted in her later work on aesthetics. During the course of the 1890s she refined the ideas which she had first developed in *Juvenilia* and incorporated them into her development of Theodor Lipps's theory of *Einfühlung* or empathy, most fully described in her later work *Beauty and Ugliness* (1912). What is more to my immediate purpose is the fact that her theoretical observations about the formation of aesthetic responses have much in common with some very familiar critical positions of the 1890s. As I have suggested, her observations seemed to underwrite at a theoretical level the practice of those 'impres-sionist' critics who were concerned with particular and highly individual responses to works of art. While Vernon Lee was a critic aware of the presuppositions which made her own critical

[26] Vernon Lee, 'Lake of Charlemagne', 61.
[27] Grant Allen, *Physiological Aesthetics* (London, 1877), 52.
[28] James Ward, 'Psychology', 70–1.

statements possible, other writers of the 1880s and 1890s were less analytical. None the less many drew quite freely upon the idea of association to explain some aspects of their own critical views. Perhaps the best example of association being used to justify relative and subjective aesthetic reactions is that made in 1894 by Lionel Johnson in his lecture on political art, 'Poetry and Patriotism'. Johnson argued that emotional reactions to political art were determined *solely* by the associations aroused by it:

> A regimental march may be very far from good music: but the first roll of the drums and shrilling of the fifes make many a man burn to be a soldier. It is simply and solely association, that has this magical effect: association can turn downright ugliness into a thing of beauty, or at the least, into something loveable.[29]

Johnson was in fact sceptical about the appropriateness of such judgements and tried to make a distinction (although not a very compelling one) between interested and disinterested criticism; but the significant point is that association is invoked with a casualness which betrays its familiarity.

However, it is the second part of Vernon Lee's essay in *Juvenilia* which is more radical and more interesting. Here it was not relative, partial, or subjective responses to art which were the issue, nor their opposite, Johnson's implausible politically or socially 'neutral' objectivity. Vernon Lee asserted that Associationism described the basis of *all* mental activity and thus provided a key to understanding both critical and creative activities. It followed, then, that the processes by which the spectator perceives and responds to a work of art were of *precisely* the same order, and thus of the same status, as the processes involved in its creation. As creation and criticism were aspects of the same mental function, so criticism could, under certain circumstances, actually become creation, or more exactly, re-creation. Vernon Lee had, that is, derived from contemporary psychological theory the same arguments which were to be made over the coming decade by some literary and art critics. In one passage from *Juvenilia*, Vernon Lee seems

---

[29] Lionel Johnson, 'Poetry and Patriotism', in W. B. Yeats and Lionel Johnson, *Poetry and Ireland* (Dundrum, 1908), 27. The essay was the text of a lecture given in Apr. 1894.

to be anticipating very accurately the justification for these critical arguments:

Similarly with the statue, one glance, just taking in the general aspect, perhaps another to see how well the stone is cut; and then you contemplate the work with that vague stare which sees nothing; you think of the hero's life, and of his mighty battle-shout, of his tears over his fallen comrade. Of the waves on the Trojan shore, the clear night over the plain dotted with watch-fires; the youth of mankind—Socrates, Sappho, the brutal Roman praetors, and a whole Panathenaic procession of impertinent associations. Meanwhile the marble stands before you, neither fighting, nor shouting, nor weeping; with no waves or watch-fires near him, and no consciousness of the youth of mankind; a mere comely, naked body, with a wisp of drapery over the arm, and no personality save in the name graven on the pedestal.[30]

The most innovative aspect of impressionist criticism was that it made a virtue of Vernon Lee's main point here. For this type of criticism, it was the *reaction to* the art-object which was of paramount importance. Indeed, that reaction was in many respects more interesting than, and certainly of equal importance to, the object in which it had its origin; as a consequence, judgements such as 'correct' or 'incorrect', and so forth, were no longer applicable, because such judgements had to be socially, and not individually, authorized. In other words, criticism had become precisely what psychological aesthetics had proposed it inevitably had to be: an affective discipline. For Oscar Wilde and for his less famous contemporaries, the functions of the creative and the critical faculties became strictly analogous; criticism existed in creation and creation in criticism. Indeed Wilde was to argue that 'the highest Criticism . . . [is] the purest form of personal impression . . . [and] in its way is more creative than creation'; moreover, the more subjective the criticism the better, for by mentally re-creating the object under contemplation, criticism aspired to be a chronicle of the experience of the critic's 'own soul'.[31] In this respect passages from Wilde's critical dialogues are at times strikingly reminiscent of Vernon Lee's arguments:

[30] Vernon Lee, 'Lake of Charlemagne', 50–1.
[31] As there is yet no reliable nor complete edition of Wilde's criticism, I shall quote from that most easily available, the one-volume Collins *Complete Works* (London, 1967). See Oscar Wilde, 'Critic As Artist', *Intentions* in *Complete Works*, 1027.

[It] is rather the beholder who lends to the beautiful thing its myriad meanings. . . . To the critic the work of art is simply a suggestion for a new work of his own, that need not necessarily bear any obvious resemblance to the thing it criticises.[32]

However, the qualification suggested by Vernon Lee's final allusion to the specificity of the 'mere comely, naked body' of the statue is important. Her sentence exposes the limitations inherent in any attempt to construct a full-blown explanation of art from observations about the psychology of either its creator or its spectators, limitations which, as I shall suggest, were in fact responsible for the ultimate marginalization of the whole tradition of impressionist criticism. The limitations of both psychological aesthetics and impressionist criticism are these: it *is* transparently true that a work of art is produced under the direction of one (or of a series) of psychological states: any human activity necessarily must be. But once the creation is complete, the work, considered as art, ceases to have any further psychological relation to its creator. Its existence becomes a public one. Considered solely as an expressive artefact, of course, the work *would* naturally still continue to have a psychological relation with its creator, but this relationship will have nothing to do with its designation or existence as art. Whatever relationships a work of art as an expressive object has to its creator, they are not considerations which can properly be said to affect its status as art. A similar case is true of the effects which art produces in an audience. Vernon Lee's statue is a work of art for reasons other than the affective states under which it was created or the affective states which it produces. Moreover, as I have suggested above, in so far as impressionist criticism rested upon a theory which described the aesthetic object rather than the art-object, it could have nothing to say about some crucial aspects of art-objects—such as their history, or the political and social circumstances in which they were produced. It was these elements which the embryonic academic and institutionalized literary criticism of the 1880s and 1890s appropriated, and which finally ensured the marginalization of impressionist criticism.

[32] Ibid. 1029–30.

PART II

CRITICAL STANCES

Literary criticism is not your forte my dear fellow. Don't try it. You should leave that to people who haven't been at a University.

Oscar Wilde, *The Importance of Being Earnest.*

the natural inability of a community corrupted by authority to understand or appreciate Individualism.

Oscar Wilde, *The Soul of Man Under Socialism.*

4

Walter Pater

In the light of my arguments about the nature of the intellectual crisis in Britain in the last three decades of the nineteenth century, it is fairly easy to see that the critical practices which characterize Aestheticism are not the isolated changes, nor its main protagonists the idiosyncratic figures, which many literary historians have taken them to be. They are part of a wider set of general phenomena which involved the institutionalization of knowledge, professionalization, and changes in the nature of intellectual authority. Hence, in this reading, it is possible to see writers such as Walter Pater and Oscar Wilde as intensely serious critics engaging with some of the most compelling intellectual issues in the late nineteenth century.

Recent cultural historians have begun to account for Pater's or Wilde's relationship with authority in terms of their reactions to the sexual politics of their time: in this view it is the primacy of sexual politics which underwrites and informs all other modes of authority.[1] In many ways it is tempting to read the lives of Pater and Wilde in this manner. Certainly, hostile reactions to them became more frequent and strident as the century progressed and that hostility increasingly identified as its target what was seen as 'aberrant' sexuality in the work of both men. Moreover, criticism over intellectual and artistic issues was frequently used as a device to disguise bitter personal attacks. But although sexual politics in the lives of Wilde and Pater is clearly important, and although it might have been the

---

[1] See e.g. Ed Cohen, 'Writing gone Wilde: Homoerotic Desire in the Closet of Representation', *PMLA*, 102 (1987), 801–13; Jonathan Dollimore, 'Different Desires: Subjectivity and Transgression in Wilde and Gide', *Textual Practice*, 1 (1987), 48–67; Richard Ellmann, *Oscar Wilde* (London, 1987); Regenia Gagnier, *Idylls of the Market-Place* (Aldershot, 1987); ead., '*De Profundis* as *Epistola: In Carcere et Vinculis*: A Materialist Reading of Oscar Wilde's Autobiography', *Criticism*, 26 (1984), 335–54; Richard Dellamora, 'Representation and Homophobia in *The Picture of Dorian Gray*', *Victorian Newsletter*, 73 (1988), 28–31.

origin of many of their later attitudes to all forms of authority, including intellectual authority, it says little about those attitudes in themselves. While it is indeed possible to see behind both Wilde's and Pater's insistence upon the autonomy and sovereignty of taste in aesthetic matters a barely disguised claim for the freedom of the individual,[2] in other areas of life Pater, unlike Wilde, chose an arena which was purely intellectual. Hence I shall discuss his career in those terms alone.

I have suggested that there was a dilemma facing serious literary critics in the 1870s and that it took the form of a crisis of authority. Neither specialized nor popular reviewing could aspire to the kind of authority which had formerly been the province of the eminent individual writer. And the consequences and implications of this state of affairs—the decline of the prestige of the individual writer and the inadequacy of *both* specialist and popular criticism—provide a useful way of surveying Pater's career as a critic.

For most of his adult life Pater taught at Brasenose College, Oxford. His early years at Oxford had been marked by some success and he earned for himself a reputation as a stylish young don. A mordantly witty agnostic, he was thought a paradoxical and entertaining conversationalist and something of an iconoclast. In the Oxford of the late 1860s and early 1870s, still a bastion of religious and moral orthodoxy, such a mixture was not without its attendant dangers. But Pater's iconoclasm had a more serious and altogether more intellectual dimension, manifested in his first book, *Studies in the History of the Renaissance* (1873). The volume was a collection of periodical essays, but the sum was more than its parts. The book is combative, the work of a young man eager to prove himself. In it, as I have suggested, Pater not only urbanely took issue with the particular judgements of his distinguished elders; he radically questioned the whole aesthetic which made those judgements possible. Pater's two specific adversaries in his essays were Matthew Arnold and John Ruskin. Indeed, the book's aesthetic is a direct engagement with the authority of Arnold's prescriptions for criticism; moreover, some of the judgements

---

[2] For different views of this idea of individualism, see Karl Miller, *Doubles* (Oxford, 1985), 221–9; Hans Mayer, *Outsiders: A Study in Life and Letters*, tr. Dennis M. Sweet (Cambridge, Mass., 1982), *passim*.

on specific works of art contained in it can be seen as a direct challenge to the authority of the opinions of Ruskin. In so far as *The Renaissance* is a challenge to the dominant critical voices of the time, it is also an attempt to relocate the authority for the assessment and appreciation of a work of art within the individual.

How did such iconoclasm work? In the first instance, the choice of the book's subject was not random. The construction and the historiography of the Renaissance were topical, and moreover were taking place within an academic milieu. Pater, of course, was a fellow of an Oxford college, but *The Renaissance* was not an academic work; indeed it eschewed most of the paraphernalia and devices of contemporary academic commentary. In Pater's study, the Renaissance is not an epoch and certainly not confined to fifteenth- and sixteenth-century Italian art. For Pater, 'renaissance' represents a mode of mental existence which recurs throughout history: indeed in *The Renaissance* it manifests itself in historical moments as diverse as that presented in the narrative of Aucassin and Nicolette and in the career and work of the eighteenth-century German historian Johann Joachim Winckelmann. It is an attribute of genius which, according to Pater's quotation from Blake in the preface 'is always above its age';[3] 'renaissance' exists as a metaphor—it is a function of the expressive sensibility of a number of artists. Thus in *The Renaissance* Pater does not discuss many specific works of art—although the prescriptions which he maintains in the preface would seem to require him to do so. Instead he tends to treat the works of a particular artist as they form themselves into a *type* or *category* of artefact. The typicality rather than the uniqueness of an artist's products is what is of interest to him. Now all of this represents a quite specific engagement with contemporary historiography of the Renaissance. Generally speaking, nineteenth-century art history tended to organize the history of art into just that—a *history*—defined in the first place by periodicity, of which the Renaissance was one such epoch; and within such periods, individual artists tended to be ranked. Pater either

---

[3] Walter Pater, *The Renaissance*, ed. Hill, p. xxi.

refuses to endorse or simply ignores all of this historical scholarship.[4]

As J. B. Bullen has pointed out, the 1860s, the decade which saw Pater's first interest in the subject, offered a variety of ways in which the notion of the Renaissance could be addressed:

Within this decade, the concept of 'renaissance' was historiographically unstable and its status as historical myth extremely problematic. Was it a historical period at all, and if so how did it stand in relation to the Middle Ages? Was it characterized by the sum total of its works in art and literature or was it more specifically a set of ideas, attitudes and values? Was it located geographically in Italy or did it extend to France and the rest of Europe? The most pertinent question, however, and the one which gave most trouble, was its relationship with modern culture. Was it, as Ruskin in England and Rio in France would have it, the source of modern materialism, infidelity and pride extending, as Ruskin put it, 'from the Grand Canal to Gower Street', or was it, as Quinet and Michelet would have it, an ontological, antinomian revolution which laid the foundations for modern rationalism and free thinking.[5]

The Renaissance treats of these issues, but only, as it were, glancingly. Problems of historiography are broached, but Pater makes no attempt to resolve them.

The Renaissance thus becomes the pattern for Pater's criticism on a number of scores. If a contemporary reader looked to it for history, for historiography, for reference to contemporary views on the subjects of the essays, for scholarly corroboration, or for archival evidence, the search would have been fruitless. The authority for the judgements for specific works of art lies in the prestige which Pater—prematurely, given his reputation at the time—claimed for *himself*. At a rhetorical level, the reader is directed by the normalizing power of the magisterial Paterian 'we', or by the constant attenuation of sentences in which the reader's power to dissent is perpetually deferred. This situation, of course, answers precisely to the polemic in the preface to

[4] For details of Pater's engagement with the views of his contemporaries, see *The Renaissance*, ed. Hill, 280–443; and J. B. Bullen 'Pater and Ruskin on Michelangelo: Two Contrasting Views', in Philip Dodd (ed.), *Walter Pater: An Imaginative Sense of Fact* (London, 1981), 55–73.

[5] J. B. Bullen, 'The Historiography of *Studies in the History of the Renaissance*', in Laurel Brake and Ian Small (eds.), *Walter Pater in the 1990s* (Greensboro, NC, forthcoming, 1991).

the book, where the case for the validity of subjective responses is argued. Pater's preface has often been noticed for the novelty of its ideas, particularly in its attempt to see in the aesthetic something quite independent of the ethical. But in one obvious sense the preface was very outdated: in the ways in which it attempts·to rehabilitate individual authority, and to disregard an institutional authority based on a scholarly consensus, it looks back to the critical writing of the 1850s. The early 1870s were probably the last years when it was possible for a writer to entertain seriously such an ambiguous attitude to intellectual authority. As I have indicated, with increasing academic specialization and the consequent decline in authority of the Victorian 'sage', matters changed quickly in the next two decades. Pater's attitude to authority, however, underwent no such profound revisions; indeed, in Pater's work all forms of textual and historical authority came under an increasingly distrusting scrutiny.

In 1882 in the *Fortnightly Review*, Grant Allen published an essay ruminating on what he called the 'Decay of Criticism'.[6] He began by reviewing an essay in the *Revue des deux mondes*, 'La Critique contemporaine et les causes de son affaiblissement', by the French academician E. Caro. Caro's subject was the decline of authoritative French criticism, and Allen used the essay to make some similar observations about the state of contemporary British literary criticism. Allen paraphrases Caro's criticism of French cultural life, but in terms so ambiguous that it is clear that he perceives their obvious applicability to Britain:

There are still critics—ay, and good ones too. But they cannot stem the tide of public taste. . . . Their authority is only recognised within a small sphere of picked intellects, and does not affect the general current of the popular mind. They have reputations, but they have not influence. . . . Judges there still are, no doubt; but a literary court there is not. The decrees of the experts lack validity. . . . Their authority is personal, not official. In short, criticism has now become a happy accident; it is no longer an institution universally accepted as

---

[6] Grant Allen, 'Decay of Criticism', *Fortnightly Review*, 37 (1882), 339–51. E. Caro's article 'Critique contemporaine et les causes de son affaiblissement', was published on 1 Feb. 1882 in *Revue des deux mondes*, 49 (1882), 547–66. Caro's essay in fact ends less pessimistically than Allen suggests: '"Pour qui donc travailler?" — Je réponderai, "Pour le vrai public et pour les vrais juges." Car il existe encore de vrais juges, intègres, incorruptibles et clairvoyans.' (565.)

of yore by virtue of its collective force and its recognised light and leading. Our generation has altered all that.[7]

While Allen was careful to make a number of distinctions between British and French cultural life, he saw British literary criticism as a discourse now dispossessed of its former authority, and his reasons for this view are revealing. In Allen's opinion, what had formerly been authoritative literary criticism in major journals had been superseded by simple reviewing. His distinction here between criticism and reviewing is an important one. On the one hand the practice of criticism implied both some kind of judgement *and* a specialist knowledge; indeed, that knowledge was precisely what distinguished and gave authority to the critic's judgements. On the other hand there was, in Allen's view, simple reviewing, which required no specialist knowledge, nor distinctive judgements, and which was thus without any kind of authority. Allen suggests that critical authority resides in both the prestige of the individual *and* in the specialist knowledge which that individual possesses, and further that this knowledge is different in kind and in quality from institutionalized knowledge. The growth of the popular press and of journalism had led to mediocrity and, '[n]aturally, reviewing thus becomes wholly unauthoritative'.[8] Moreover, academic reviewing had become institutionalized, specialized, and thus narrow, for 'specialism is full of attractions for mediocrity':

Who has not met in London the man who greets any mention of a Darwin, a Spencer, or a Helmholtz with the stereotyped remark, 'Well, for my part, I can't say what his general theories may be worth, but I can certainly assert that in my own department, his molecular physics, you know, are horribly shaky,' or 'his views about Amharic grammar are painfully false,' or, 'his information as to the edicts of Asoka is not corroborated by the latest German researches.'[9]

Between these two opposed practices there was no longer room for the educated, authoritative literary critic to operate; there was simply no place for the kind of subjective criticism which Pater had attempted to practise in *The Renaissance*. (It is worth noting that the situation which Allen describes is in fact remarkably similar to that depicted by George Gissing in *New*

[7] Allen, 'Decay of Criticism', 340–1.   [8] Ibid. 348.   [9] Ibid. 350.

Grub Street in 1891.) If this analysis is in outline correct, then much of Pater's writing in the 1880s and 1890s can be seen in terms of an engagement with the different forms of authority then being discussed. Allen's essay, for example, begs the whole question of the nature of authority in *literary* discourse: the two kinds of authority which he identifies, the popular and the academic, said nothing about the manner in which texts were authorized. It is precisely this context which allows the real significance of Pater's writing in the 1880s and early 1890s to be seen, for his ambition was always to engage with, and to attempt to redefine, many of the forms of intellectual authority. *Marius the Epicurean* and *Plato and Platonism* are two examples of such a strategy. In different ways they are works which contest contemporary concepts of authority. Although *Marius the Epicurean* is fiction, it is a form of fiction which enabled Pater to continue a critical interrogation of literary, historical, aesthetic, and philosophical topics. (Indeed we have Pater's own sanction for reading the novel in this manner, for in a famous footnote to the third edition of *The Renaissance*, he referred the reader to *Marius*, where he had 'dealt more fully' with 'the thoughts suggested' by the conclusion.[10]

Marius is a novel dense with allusion, quotation, and citation. In the nature and the uses of these devices, Pater's attitudes to authority—historical, scholarly, and textual—become strikingly evident. For the sake of brevity, a few examples will have to stand for the tendency of the whole book. In the web of intertextual relationships established in *Marius*, the most important and the most immediate field of reference results from allusion to, or quotation from, a wide body of classical literature. Many of the details of Roman life are taken from literary sources, such as the letters of Pliny or of Fronto, but the resulting picture is not like that usually encountered in the imaginative historical novel of the time. Contemporary historical novelists tended to use source-material to provide authenticating background details. For Pater, however, that source-material, especially when it concerned the authority of competing philosophical or religious systems, became the very substance of the novel itself. However, in a work which deals

---

[10] *The Renaissance*, ed. Hill, 186.

with the nature of the differences between revealed religion and natural religion, or between various ethical systems, the manner in which texts are authorized, and the nature of authority itself, are indeed crucial topics. It is not far-fetched to suggest that the authorization of texts, especially that of the supremely authorized text, the Bible, is in many ways the subject of the novel. The attitude which Pater adopts towards his source-material gives *Marius* its originality and its modernity. The author who plays with authority—the re-emergence of the iconoclastic author of *The Renaissance*—is what distinguishes Pater's work from that of his Victorian contemporaries. That challenge to authority is subtle, but it is cumulative in its effect; and it is always directed at the educated reader.

The subversiveness of *Marius* exists in its intertextuality and its quotations. However, for Pater, quotation and citation, and the manner in which they embody textual authority, were not simple, undifferentiated concepts. Pater uses quotation in three quite distinct ways, each of which marks off his attitude to authority as something quite novel in the 1880s. The first, and the easiest to recognize, is his use of a short interpolated quotation. These references direct the educated reader to certain aspects of Roman culture and to known and established facts of Roman history. Some, like the opening reference to Numa,[11] would have been so familiar to Pater's audience that they would pass as a part of the general knowledge of an educated man. Other quotations are used in a manner which typified contemporary scholarship, namely as supporting or corroborative evidence for learning. The first examples of this sort of quotation come slightly later in the first chapter and are taken from Tibullus and from Virgil respectively:

> At mihi contingat patrios celebrare Penates,
> Reddereque antiquo menstrua thura Lari.

> Candidus insuetum miratur limen Olympi,
> Sub pedibusque videt nubes et sidera.[12]

---

[11] See id., *Marius the Epicurean*, ed. Ian Small (Oxford, 1986), 3. The first chapter carries the title 'The Religion of Numa'.

[12] The first quotation is Tibullus, 1. iii. 33–4: 'But may it be my lot to celebrate the Penates and make monthly offering to the ancient Lar'. The quotation from Virgil is taken from the *Eclogues*, v. 56–7: 'In beauty he marvels at the threshold of Olympus, not known before, and sees the clouds and stars beneath his feet.' See Pater, *Marius*, 3, 7.

Scholarly quotation or citation in these instances becomes historical verification, in a manner which would have been familiar to contemporary classical scholars. With this sort of textual reference, Pater is always careful to indicate the source of his quotation as well as the manner in which it is being used as authority. Indeed on two occasions he actually uses footnotes to do so—Pater's novel has about the same number of footnotes as *The Renaissance* or *Plato and Platonism*.

Throughout the novel, however, there is a second type of quotation which is deeply embedded in the text and which works as a kind of allusion. On these occasions, Pater clearly expects his readers to be familiar with the sources he is referring them to; and the main source is the Bible. Passages from the Psalms, the Sapiental books, Pater's own translations of hymns or of ancient liturgical material, are all located in the text without any pointers to the manner of their use, or indeed to their origin. Scriptural discourse, unlike the discourse of classical literatures, is not marked off textually in any way. Although his readers would have been much more familiar with the Bible, hymns, and liturgical material than their twentieth-century counterparts, Pater's refusal to signal or to discriminate between orders of authority is in fact much more unsettling than it at first appears. It is not simply that Latin and Greek quotation and citation are being set against biblical quotation of known and established doctrinal significance; Pater's use of religious authority is itself no simple matter. In the first place, religious authority in *Marius* is not simply biblical in origin.[13] Quotations from Proverbs, for example, and the apocryphal Book of Wisdom are set against each other. Pater's use of biblical authority elides the doctrinal distinctions to be made between each text. In this respect it should perhaps be added

---

[13] Complex uses of allusive quotation are to be found in chs. 18 and 21, where Pater's sources include his own translations of a hymn, the Sapiental books of the Bible and Aurelius' *Meditations*. What is important, though, is obviously *not* the origins of the quotations, but the fact that they come to the reader dislocated from their original contexts, with no qualification about the vastly different nature of their liturgical, biblical, or philosophical authority. It may have been Pater's intention here to point to the similarities between biblical and Stoic doctrine, or to illustrate how one informs the other. As I indicate, such a strategy would certainly have been entirely consistent with the uses made of the *Meditations* by some of his contemporaries. But the effect of juxtapositions of material such as that quoted above is of quite a different order, for the distinctions between the different nature of the authority of each text are simply lost.

that Pater is following a not unfamiliar nineteenth-century practice. But he employs a further and wholly untypical strategy: he sets both passages against a series of further quotations from Marcus Aurelius' *Meditations*, and thus what marks off the distinctive authority of each is placed in jeopardy.

However, the range of Pater's quotation from religious authorities is wider than merely that of the Bible or the Apocrypha.[14] Religious citation or quotation in nineteenth-century fictional discourse tends to work in a fairly simple manner, principally and obviously as the highest form of moral authority which the writer can invoke. But in *Marius* both the manner and the range of religious quotation and reference tend to controvert this simple notion of authority: the severely orthodox and the strangely heterodox are played against each other. The result is oddly unsettling, in that in the very play of discourse the nature of textual authority is undermined or eroded; and finally the nature of authority itself is challenged.

Pater's use of quotation does not exist simply at the level of the interpolated line of Latin or Greek poetry or the unattributed verse from the Bible, the Apocrypha, or early liturgies. At key points in the work Pater translates, reorders—in fact rewrites—whole discourses. And it is at these points in the novel that we encounter Pater's most profound engagement with the notion of the authority of texts, and with intellectual authority itself. Some of the sources of the material which Pater translates or rewrites are well known; but others are well-enough disguised still to deceive otherwise well-informed critics. For brevity, a few examples will have to stand as representative of much of the novel: first, three apparently unconnected quotations from, or allusions to, Goethe and to St John; secondly, a fictional 'oration' which Pater attributes to the historically real Cornelius Fronto, but which is in fact composed of his own thoughts and paraphrases from Aurelius' *Meditations*; and thirdly, Pater's use of the anonymous *Historia Augusta* as a source. In all these instances, the problem of textual authority has a further dimension—that of the mediation of texts. So in

---

[14] There is also an eclectic, and so, in a sense, rewritten set of quotations from the 2nd-cent. apostolic father Hermas; and, most strangely, a reference to a description of hell in the work of the American Calvinist Jonathan Edwards: disturbingly, these are all set one against the other.

the novel the reader finds three apparently unconnected quotations or allusions—to *Faust*, to *Wilhelm Meister*, and to the New Testament. The exact passages are as follows:

[T]hat eternal process of nature, of which at a later time Goethe spoke as the 'Living Garment', whereby God is seen of us, ever in weaving at the 'Loom of Time'.

America is here and now:—here, or nowhere: as Wilhelm Meister finds out one day.

[R]ather of one who gives a meaning of his own, yet a very real one, to those old words—*Let us work while it is day!*[15]

The ultimate sources for these references are *Faust*, I. i. 155–6; *Wilhelm Meisters Lehrjahre*, book 7, Chapter 3, and John 9: 4. But the immediate source appears to be Thomas Carlyle's *Sartor Resartus*, where they appear in a form much closer to Pater's formulations than to the original works. Where Pater *does* indicate a textual origin, ironically, and confusingly, it is to the ultimate rather than the mediating source.

The other important point to note here is that the *status* of these and other quoted materials in the work differs quite significantly. An example of this tendency is to be found in chapter 15, where Pater describes the Roman Stoic and orator Cornelius Fronto delivering a discourse on 'The Nature of Morals'. From the textual signals in the novel, there is no way in which even the most careful reader may detect that Fronto's discourse is less authoritative or less 'real' than *Faust* or *Wilhelm Meisters Lehrjahre*. Of course Cornelius Fronto *was* historically real enough: indeed in the course of the novel Pater often quotes from his correspondence with Marcus Aurelius, and on one occasion actually refers to the authenticating source of that correspondence, its discovery in Milan by Cardinal Mai in 1815. 'The Nature of Morals', however, *does not exist*; nor is there any record of the discourse ever having existed. But the 'fictionality' of Fronto's oration is never acknowledged. I use the term 'fictionality' guardedly because Fronto's alleged address is in fact composed of material derived from Aurelius' *Meditations*, but in a way which substantially edits and reorders it. In a work of fiction no author is, of course, obliged to respect

---

[15] Pater, *Marius*, 74, 80, 155.

truth-values, or to attribute texts correctly. But Pater's novel is marked by its inconsistency. The absence of any authorizing signals in the text which would consistently indicate the nature of such knowing misattributions is one of Pater's most unsettling textual devices.

A further problem exists in the nature of the translations of some of the novel's sources. For instance, Pater takes a cavalier attitude to the weight of authoritative intellectual and academic opinion in the way he treats one of his main sources for details of Roman public and political life, the pseudonymous *Scriptores Historiae Augustae*. His use of this particular source reveals a great deal about his knowledge of, and attitudes to, classical learning in the years between 1885, when *Marius the Epicurean* was first published, and his death in 1894. There is no doubt that Pater knew the *Historia Augusta* very well. He refers to it by name in the course of the novel, and incorporates into the text many small quotations from it. He also includes translations of ten substantial episodes from the *Vitae* of Antoninus Pius and Marcus Antoninus. The cumulative effect of these references is to give the impression that Pater thought the *Historia* reliable and accurate in its accounts of Roman political life. Such an impression is reinforced by the fact that while most of these passages were revised between the first (1885) and third (1892) editions of the novel, those revisions were all stylistic: for Pater, the authenticity of the *Historia* remained intact. This in itself is strange. In the years between the publication of those editions, the authenticity of the *Historia* was indeed seriously questioned in two essays in *Hermes*, in which Hermann Dessau contested the then dominant views about the work's dating and authorship. Pater seems to have been either totally ignorant of, or totally uninterested in, the dimensions of this debate and the resulting controversy.[16] In fact, the passages in *Marius* where Pater is most unwilling to trust completely the authority of the *Historia* seem to depend not on the latest scholarship, but on an edition of the *Historia* by the German scholar Hermann Peter in 1865. Peter

---

[16] See Hermann Dessau, 'Über Zeit und Persönlichkeit der S.H.A.', *Hermes*, 24 (1889), 337–92; id., 'Über die S.H.A.', *Hermes*, 27 (1892), 561–605. For details of Pater's references to, and quotations from, the *Historia*, see Ian Small, '*Marius the Epicurean* and the *Historia Augusta*', *Notes and Queries*, 34 (1987), 48–50. See also Sir Ronald Syme, *Ammianus and the Historia Augusta* (Oxford, 1968), 176–91.

disputes the authority of exactly those passages in the *Vita* of Marcus Antoninus which Pater also most explicitly distrusts.[17] The logic of the treatment of sources such as the *Historia* and the *Meditations* is simple: Pater was deeply interested and widely read in contemporary debate and research; but in most matters of historiography he was unwilling to seek in or grant to that academic community a final intellectual authority.[18]

There is one last consequence of this playing with the status of discourses. In the novel, source-material ranges from the self-declaredly fictional (as with the reference to Lucius' metamorphosis into an ass in Pater's adaptation of Apuleius' *The Golden Ass*) to what Pater held to be demonstrably and horrifyingly true (in Eusebius' account of the death of Christian martyrs in his *Ecclesiastical History*). But when the reader encounters this latter narrative, the ability to identify it as 'true' has been jeopardized by Pater's consistent erosion of the standards of textual authority whereby such judgements may be made. By this stage in the novel the reader has lost what had hitherto been considered a crucial critical privilege: the ability to organize the discourses in a text into a pattern which

[17] These include references to the conduct of Aurelius' family, esp. to the plague and Lucius Verus' actions in the Parthian wars; to the circumstances surrounding the death of Lucius; to the infidelity of Faustina; and to the death of Annius Verus. See Pater, *Marius*, 4, 63, 71, 109, 125, 135, 157, 173–5.

[18] It seems that in his treatment of Marcus Aurelius' *Meditations* in *Marius*, Pater was once more attempting to controvert a growing academic orthodoxy. The popularity of the *Meditations* was not new in the late 19th cent. Historiographers of Rome such as B. G. Niebuhr and Theodor Mommsen, of whom Pater would have been well aware, saw in Aurelius a model of classical virtue. For Niebuhr it was 'more delightful to speak of M Aurelius than of any man; for, if there is any sublime human virtue, it is his'; and *The Meditations* was a 'golden book' (B. G. Niebuhr, *Lectures on Roman History*, tr. H. M. Chepmell and F. C. Demmler (London, 1855), iii. 237–8). In the later decades of the century *The Meditations* were seen as broadly endorsing the ethics of 19th-cent. Anglicanism but not its dogma. In the 1870s and 1880s popular British historians and essayists, such as W. W. Capes, William Wallace, and W. W. Story, dwelt upon the relevance of Stoicism for the contemporary mind, and editions of Meric Causabon's and Jeremy Collier's famous 17th- and 18th-cent. translations were frequently reprinted. (See e.g. W. W. Capes, *Stoicism* (London, 1880); William Wallace, *Epicureanism* (London, 1880); W. W. Story, 'Conversation with Marcus Aurelius', *Fortnightly Review*, NS 13 (1873), 178–96; Frederick Pollock, 'Marcus Aurelius and the Stoic Philosophy', *Mind*, 4 (1879), 47–68.) *Marius the Epicurean* is a contribution to this debate about the contemporary relevance of Aurelius' Stoicism, but it is also a controversion and repudiation of it. For details of Pater's engagement with this contemporary scholarship, see Ian Small, 'Annotating "Hard" Nineteenth Century Novels', *Essays in Criticism*, 36 (1986), 281–93; id., 'Editing Pater', *English Literature In Transition*, 30 (1987), 213–18.

discriminates truth and fictionality through the attribution of textual authority.

In all this we are presented with a spectrum of quoted material which in fact comprises a large proportion of the novel's overall length. At one end of that spectrum is the faithful translating of an authorized, identified, and attributed work; at the other is the rewriting of a text which has been denied its authorship by an historically existent character and ascribed to another historically existent character. What is clear from all these examples is that one of Pater's principal intellectual concerns was to engage with concepts of textual and historiographical authority. Authority, for Pater, resides in the individual: the authority of an utterance, whether critical or fictional (and it is interesting in this respect that Pater's writing constantly elides the distinctions to be made between genres and between modes of writing) depends upon the authority of the individual making the utterance, and not upon any consistent or verifiable adducing of 'evidence'. Were such tactics restricted to *The Renaissance* or to *Marius*, it could be argued that they are to be explained either by Pater's youth or by the fact that he was writing fiction. But the tactics persist throughout his career, up to his most clearly 'academic' work—and his last book to be published in his lifetime—*Plato and Platonism* (1893).

Plato and Platonism is a version of a series of lectures on Plato which Pater gave at Oxford formally in the early 1890s, but perhaps also gave on a less formal basis in the late 1880s. As lectures, that is, they had a specific academic context. In fact, when Pater came to write *Plato and Platonism* he had a very strong tradition of academic and scholarly writing on Plato to define himself against; it was moreover a tradition which amounted to an orthodoxy. *The Renaissance* too was written against, almost in defiance of, a tradition of scholarly or academic authority. But in the two decades between Pater's first book and his last, as I have suggested, forms of authority other than those represented by academic institutions had become increasingly difficult to invoke. University reforms had been implemented and the process of increasing institutionalization and specialization mentioned in earlier chapters was well under way. Thus whereas it might have been possible for Pater's criticism to be both unscholarly *and* serious in 1873, such a combination became increasingly less possible in the years up to 1893. The critical reception of *Plato and Platonism*, and the subsequent judging of it against an orthodoxy of Platonic scholarship, indicates how removed the subjective, 'impressionist' criticism of Pater had become from the arenas of contemporary academic debate. The most competent accounts of the book were the brief notice in *Mind* (in April 1893)[19] and the detailed review by Lewis Campbell, a pupil of Jowett, a long-standing acquaintance of Pater, and professor of Greek at St Andrews, in the *Classical Review* (in June 1893). Both reviews, like those by Edmund Gosse, Richard Holt Hutton, Arthur Symons, and Richard Le Gallienne, evince an admiration for the work; but the grounds for that admiration are revealing. Gosse had admired the book as the work of a 'scrupulous craftsman in prose'; for Campbell Dodgson the book was 'so full of beauty'; and for Lewis Campbell, Pater was a 'poet'. Such characterizations are significant, because they shift the grounds upon which the book was to be judged. If the book could be seen in the first instance as 'literary', then the conditions governing scholarly writing, which Pater had clearly ignored, simply did not apply. Indeed, most reviewers, when they discussed Pater's scholarship, noted his ignorance of contemporary research. Typically, and, in the light of his own treatment at the hands of Churton Collins in the previous decade, understandably, Edmund Gosse tried in this respect to make a virtue of necessity:

Yet those who are interested in pure literature as in itself a delightful form of artistic discipline may well claim that a book composed with a conscious regard to form should not be shut off altogether from their consideration, because it deals with a subject primarily associated with non-artistic branches of intellectual labour. It is becoming a serious misfortune that specialisation tends more and more in each generation to exile from the province of pure literature all themes which deal directly with facts, or require exact definition.[20]

Gosse was addressing the issue, but by blurring it, had mis-stated the problem. Critical writing could, by 1893, still be

---

[19] The notice in *Mind* was anonymous. See *Mind*, NS 2 (1893), 251.
[20] See Edmund Gosse, *New Review*, 8 (1893); repr. in R. M. Seiler (ed.), *Walter Pater: The Critical Heritage* (London, 1980), 249.

'literary', and therefore be authoritative on that ground, as reviews of Pater's work amply testified; but it could not at the same time also specify knowledge or scholarship as the grounds for its authority. In other words, the 'literary' and the 'scholarly' had by now tended to embody opposing values. Lewis Campbell dwelt upon this very issue: if Pater's appeal could not be to scholarship, it had to be to the literary sensibility:

The *matter* of the book before us has, much of it, been common property for about forty years, commencing from the time when the historic method was first seriously applied to criticism. But it is not the less a solid gain to possess this bright and genial exposition of truths which we have long potently believed. For, however he may try to veil his gift, Mr Pater is essentially a poet.[21]

Campbell's emphasis was on Pater's 'exposition'; *Plato and Platonism* was, that is, to be judged in terms of style, not scholarship—by the literary taste of *cognoscenti*, not by a community of scholars.

By the 1890s, traditions of Platonic scholarship in Britain were powerfully entrenched within academic institutions; they had originated in Oxford, principally from the work of Benjamin Jowett. In 1876 Jowett had published his enormously successful *The Republic of Plato*. Of all the commentaries on Plato in the 1880s and 1890s—and there were a great many—Jowett's was the most important because it was the most influential. It represented also the culmination of a line of scholarship which maintained a strong if inconsistent opposition to Pater's own claims as a scholar. The contrast between Jowett's introduction to his translation of *The Republic* and *Plato and Platonism* demonstrates once more Pater's cavalier attitude to matters of textual and historical scholarship. Jowett's edition was intended to form part of a comprehensive account of *The Dialogues*; its purpose was to point to the relevance of Plato for contemporary philosophical speculation. The intentions of Jowett in his first edition of *The Republic*, then, were not dissimilar to those of Pater in his discussion of Plato. But by the time he came to prepare a second edition in 1881, Jowett had become increasingly aware of the problems posed by historical and textual scholarship, which had been recently highlighted

<hr>

[21] Lewis Campbell, in *Classical Review*, 7 (1893); see Seiler (ed.), *Walter Pater*, 272.

by German academics and intellectuals. Jowett's arguments in the second edition became more restricted in scope and more closely supported by scholarly apparatus. The historical conditions surrounding the writing of *The Dialogues* figure much more centrally in his introduction. Jowett's second edition of *The Republic of Plato*, that is, was in general terms conforming to the changing requirements being made of contemporary scholarly and academic writing.

The influence of Jowett upon the main lines of Platonic criticism was enormous. Commentators in the 1890s such as Bernard Bosanquet described George Grote, Eduard Zeller, and Benjamin Jowett as the most important and authoritative recent textual and historical scholars. Indeed, Bosanquet maintained that 'the late Master of Balliol was almost the founder of a genuine philosophical study of Plato in England, even for scholars'.[22] There is ample evidence for Bosanquet's claim. The most spectacular example of Jowett's and thus Balliol's influence upon classical scholarship is the sheer number of texts which were edited by Jowett's pupils or which referred the reader back to Jowett's editions. So, for instance, in a volume of essays on Greek subjects entitled *Hellenica* (1880), all the contributors show some dependence upon Jowett's work and most were Balliol men.[23] Even though men such as Richard Nettleship, Evelyn Abbott, and Lewis Campbell (pupils or colleagues of Jowett, that is) would naturally have followed the general drift of his ideas, his influence upon other commentators depended upon the prestige of his scholarship, not on the power of either his personality or his institutional position.

Jowett's work, although enormously influential, was only the most visible mark in a wide landscape. Between 1865 and 1890 there was a significant increase in the number of editions of Plato generally available, and a sizeable increase too in the number of commentaries on *The Dialogues*. There were three main translations: William Whewell's edition in 1859, Henry Cary's edition of 1888, and finally Jowett's, which remained the

---

[22] Bernard Bosanquet, *Companion to Plato's Republic* (London, 1895), pref. Bosanquet's was perhaps the most detailed and scholarly work then available in English. In it *Plato and Platonism* finds only a footnote, in itself interesting evidence of the process of marginalization of non-scholarly forms of critical discourse which I have described.

[23] See Evelyn Abbott (ed.), *Hellenica* (London, 1880).

standard work until well after his death. Accompanying this increase in the general availability of texts there went a new awareness of recent German research into the pre-Socratic philosophers, so much so that by 1889 the American translator of Ingram Bywater's *The Fragments of Heraclitus* could devote most of his introduction to German scholarship.[24] Apart from Hegel's general account of Greek philosophy and Schleiermacher's work on Heraclitus and the pre-Socratics, the years between 1860 and 1880 saw the production of a formidable body of scholarship: the work not only of Zeller, but also Ferdinand Lassalle, Paul Schuster and, later, Edmund Pfleiderer.[25] British scholars only slowly became aware of the implications of this work; and so comparable works in Britain were later and fewer: A. W. Benn's *The Greek Philosophers* and Lewis Campbell's *The Theaetetus of Plato* in the early 1880s.[26] There was a distinct increase of interest in Greek studies in English universities, and accompanying that increase was a new scholarly rigour. The general tendency was to elaborate upon the work of Grote and Zeller, and in particular on that of Jowett; the main agents in this dissemination of ideas were scholars like James Adam, Richard Jebb, and F. W. Bussell (who was Pater's contemporary at Brasenose). Broadly this tradition of scholarship followed Jowett's lead by insisting upon discussing Socrates as a literary character and thus upon the importance of dialectic in *The Dialogues*. Then in the late 1880s and 1890s, when the work of German scholars into Plato's

[24] G. T. W. Patrick, tr., *Fragments of the Work of Heraclitus . . . on Nature: Translated from the Greek Text of Bywater . . .* (Baltimore, 1889).

[25] See *Platons Werke*, ed. Friedrich Schleiermacher (Berlin, 1817–28); Eduard Zeller, *Philosophie der Griechen* (Tübingen, 1844–52); Ferdinand Lassalle, *Philosophie Herakleitos des Dunkeln von Ephesos* (Berlin, 1858); Paul Schuster, *Über die erhaltenen Porträts der Griechischen Philosophen* (Leipzig, 1876); Edmund Pfleiderer, *Philosophie des Heraklit von Ephesus im Lichte der Mysterienidee* (Berlin, 1886).

[26] See A. W. Benn, *Greek Philosophers* (2 vols., London, 1882); Lewis Campbell, *Theaetetus of Plato* (1861; 2nd edn., London, 1883). Other contemporary works on the subject included: J. Adam (ed.), *Apology of Plato* (London, 1887); id. (ed.), *Crito of Plato* (London, 1888), id. (ed.), *Republic of Plato* (London, 1897); Ingram Bywater (ed.), *Heracliti Ephesii Reliquiae* (Oxford, 1877); A. B. Cook, *Metaphysical Basis of Plato's Ethics* (Cambridge, 1895); J. Llewelyn Davies and D. J. Vaughan (eds.), *Republic of Plato* (2nd edn., London, 1886); G. T. Kingdon, *Essay on the Protagoras of Plato* (Cambridge, 1875); A. M. Luscombe and F. J. Newnham, *Republic of Plato* (London, 1886); J. A. Towle (ed.), *Protagoras of Plato* (London, 1889); Thomas Taylor (ed.), *Republic of Plato* (London, 1894); G. H. Wells (ed.), *Euthyphro of Plato* (London, 1880); id. (ed.), *Euthydemus of Plato* (London, 1881), id. (ed.), *Republic of Plato* (London, 1886).

predecessors had become more fully appreciated and assimilated, commentators began advancing cautions about the
necessity of discussing *The Dialogues* within the context of the
history of philosophy, and arguing for the necessity for historiographical and textual research in general. There is, moreover,
another aspect to the context of *Plato and Platonism*. Alongside
the institutionalization and increased specialization of research
within British universities went an enormous increase in general interest in Plato. His work appeared in very cheap
translations and in popular editions.[27] There were also substantial numbers of paperback texts available and a significant
number of editions aimed specifically at school audiences.[28]
Within the limits which inevitably obtained for all philosophical writing, Plato had become a popular author with a
wide and varied readership.

Thus the situation which Grant Allen had noted in literary
criticism in the 1880s—the divergence of authoritative critical
writing into either academic specialism or popular journalism
—had become firmly established. There were quite distinct
audiences for the prospective writer to address, but for those
works which sought prestige principally for the knowledge
which they embodied, there was now only one form of authority
which could be invoked—that of the scholarly community.
The significant point about *Plato and Platonism* is that Pater
addresses neither audience specifically and invokes no community of scholarly authority. *Plato and Platonism* has no
supporting scholarly apparatus. Quotations, even from *The
Dialogues*, are never adequately or properly identified: indeed,
some contain errors. No reference is made to the work of other
scholars: the single exception is Pater's reference to Carl
Otfried Mueller's work in the 1820s in his chapter
'Lacedaemon', a work which as Lewis Campbell noted, was

---

[27] Selections from the *Dialogues* were printed in cheap series such as the Oxford
Translations of the Classics, Macmillan's Golden Treasury, Rivington's Educational
Lists, Kelly's Classical Keys, Bohn's Library, and Sir John Lubbock's Hundred Books.

[28] Here once again the list of editions, but more often translations, aimed exclusively
at a school readership is long. See e.g. Arthur Sidgwick, *Easy Selections from the Dialogues
of Plato* (London, 1888); G. H. Powell, *Plato's Defence of Socrates* (London, 1882); or
anon. *Talks with Plato About Life* (1887). Lewis Campbell made a selection of Jowett's
writings on Plato in 1902 and Jowett himself had contributed a preface to an edition by
John Purves (a former Balliol man) which was entitled *Selections from the Dialogues of
Plato* (London, 1883).

extremely dated by the 1890s.[29] The whole tradition of British scholarship which had grown up because of, and around, the work of Jowett is silently ignored, as if it had never existed. Now it is possible to argue that such a silence is in part a consequence of the personal antagonism between Pater and Jowett;[30] but it seems more likely that there is another, less personal explanation.

In *Plato and Platonism* authority is as vexed an issue as it is in *Marius the Epicurean*. In it, as in the earlier books, there is a set of submerged references and self-references. In *Critical Kit-Kats* (1897), Edmund Gosse described how Pater wrote surrounded by a mass of quotations and references, freed, as it were, from any defining context:

> He read with a box of these squares [of paper] beside him, jotting down on each, very roughly, anything in his author which struck his fancy, either giving an entire quotation, or indicating a reference, or noting a disposition. He did not begin, I think, any serious critical work without surrounding himself by dozens of these little loose notes. When they were not direct references or citations, they were of the nature of a *memoria technica*.[31]

A writing practice such as this accounts perfectly for the textual fabric of works such as *Marius* and *Plato and Platonism*, where the reader is all but overwhelmed by unattributed quotation, self-quotation, and reference. William Shuter has described how *Plato and Platonism* is itself a tissue of quotation from, and reference to, Pater's own earlier work:

> The reader who comes to *Plato and Platonism* from a study of Pater's other works may be forgiven for thinking it a reshuffled version of his earlier texts. Such a reader recognizes much that he has encountered before.[32]

---

[29] Pater refers to 'K. O. Müller in his laborious, yet, in spite of its air of coldness, passably romantic work on *The Dorians*'; see id., *Plato and Platonism* (London, 1910), 199–200; see also Carl Otfried Mueller, *Geschichten Hellenischer Stamme und Städte* (3 vols., Breslau, 1820–4); see esp. vols. ii and iii.

[30] As indeed I, among others, have done. See Ian Small, 'Plato and Pater: Fin-de-Siècle Aesthetics', *British Journal of Aesthetics*, 12 (1972), 369–83.

[31] Edmund Gosse, *Critical Kit-Kats* (London, 1896), 263; quoted in William F. Shuter, 'Pater's Reshuffled Text, *Nineteenth Century Literature*, 31 (1989), 502.

[32] Shuter, 'Pater's Reshuffled Text', 503. The idea of self-quotation is also addressed by Richard Bizot, 'Pater in Transition', *Philological Quarterly*, 52 (1973), 129–41.

Shuter goes on to list almost fifty repetitions of themes, of historical movements or characters, and of tropes or locutions, all taken from Pater's earlier published work.[33] The most clearly invoked reference or authority, then, is Pater himself. Explicitly and implicitly, Pater becomes his own authority. The rightness of any specific judgement resides not in textual nor historical evidence, nor in the corroborative support of a discipline of knowledge, but in Pater's own presence, or in the presence of his earlier writing in his work. Pater's prestige lies in 'Pater', for the presence of his other work in his own text, taken with the absence of reference to other validating sources, is the quality of *Plato and Platonism* which marks it off from all other contemporary writing on the same subject.

Pater was thus attempting to undertake the kind of critical enterprise which Grant Allen had insisted a decade earlier was no longer possible. In *Marius the Epicurean* and *Plato and Platonism* he was trying to write works in which and for which authority existed in the author alone. As I have indicated, by 1893 such a tactic had become beset by problems. But such a characterization explains the reception of *Plato and Platonism*; it could be welcomed as a work of art, because it eschewed the rigour and paraphernalia of scholarship—it did not, that is, announce itself as containing scholarly knowledge. At the same time, academic reviewers could point to the book's scholarly shortcomings, but could do so safe in the knowledge that Pater manifestly had had no intention of writing a work of scholarship.

[33] Shuter, 'Pater's Reshuffled Text', 503–4.

5

Oscar Wilde

Wilde inherited two quite separate traditions of authority which may be summed up in terms of the opposition between the Victorian sage and 'institutional man'. In a typically iconoclastic strategy, the former tradition, which was by the 1890s virtually defunct, Wilde attempted to revive; and the latter, which by then was dominant, Wilde attempted to overturn. The reasons for his chosen strategy can be stated very briefly. The transition from the 1870s and early 1880s, when Pater was writing and when there was still some debate about the nature of authority, to the new orthodoxy of the 1890s, when Wilde produced all of his major work, was virtually complete. By the early 1890s there was more or less a consensus that intellectual authority resided in an academic or scholarly community, and there was a consensus also about the methods and apparatus deemed appropriate both for the verification of scholarly discourse, and for invoking intellectual authority, methods which included citation, quotation, and so forth. As earlier chapters have indicated, the processes of professionalization and specialization were much more developed in the 1890s than in the 1870s. Such an observation explains a fairly constant element in contemporary criticism of Wilde—that he was a dilettante and that his work, whatever local felicities it might possess, was marred by its fundamental lack of seriousness. Rather than being a criticism, however, such an observation characterizes Wilde's intentions exactly. By the 1890s, the notion of seriousness, which Wilde's critics were citing, involved the values of specialization and of élitism which professionalization had encouraged, because by then professionalization had redefined what seriousness meant. And against the professional—and, by the 1890s, the academic—valorization of seriousness (so defined), of exclusiveness, and of specialization, Wilde set a desire to be popular. (Indeed contemptuous criticism of the burgeoning professional classes —from university-educated literary critics in *The Importance of Being Earnest* to stockbrokers in *The Picture of Dorian Gray*—was one of his constant themes.) Moreover, after the 1870s the progressive emphasis upon scholarly rigour necessarily removed mainstream intellectual activity from a public domain and placed it instead in a private academic milieu with its new and strictly defined standards of intellectual authority. So the figure of Wilde as populist can be explained in part in terms of a *strategic* reaction against this new equation which identified intellectual value with scholarly seriousness and with the restricted practices of academic institutions. And it is worth recalling in this respect that Wilde, despite a successful career at Oxford which included the Newdigate Prize for his poem 'Ravenna' and a first-class degree, failed to secure the third of his ambitions, a fellowship at Magdalen. By his stance as a populist, Wilde was reinvoking (and necessarily by this time, also exaggerating) the authority of the Victorian 'sage', for only such a strategy presented the possibility of divorcing intellectual seriousness from the confines of academic scholarship. As Wilde became more popular, and as the idea of popularity became more and more attractive to him, the tensions in his career as a writer exemplify the contradictions of such a strategy.

In a cancelled passage from an early draft of the second act of *A Woman of No Importance*, Lord Illingworth invites his illegitimate son Gerald Arbuthnot to retire to the terrace, to 'smoke a cigarette together and settle our plans for the future. A cigarette, as someone says, is the perfect type of the perfect pleasure. It is exquisite and leaves one unsatisfied. What more can one want?'[1] The irony of the passage is that the unattributed quotation is from Wilde himself, both from *The Picture of Dorian Gray* and from *Intentions*. Although disguised or elusive self-citation such as this *is* unusual for Wilde, self-borrowing does

---

[1] See Oscar Wilde, *A Woman of No Importance*, ed. Ian Small, in Oscar Wilde, *Two Society Comedies*, ed. Ian Small and Russell Jackson (London, 1983), 72. The unattributed quotation is from Lord Henry Wotton. See Oscar Wilde, *The Picture of Dorian Gray*, ed. Isobel Murray (Oxford, 1979), 79. The quotation also occurs in a slightly modified form in *Intentions*: see Oscar Wilde, *Complete Works* (London, 1967) (henceforth *CW*), 1019.

not in itself distinguish these lines in any way, for the play contains an abundance of quotation from the earlier novel. In fact, most of Lord Illingworth's sentiments are rehearsed by Lord Henry Wotton in *Dorian Gray*: an observant audience would have noticed the self-referentiality; indeed many reviewers did. Now if the relationship between *A Woman of No Importance* and *Dorian Gray* were an isolated case, then Wilde's repetition of his joke would be easy enough to explain in terms of his biography. But such self-plagiarism is anything but unique in Wilde's career; in fact, it is the rule rather than the exception. So, for example, the textual history of the last two plays, *An Ideal Husband* and *The Importance of Being Earnest*, reveals Wilde moving blocks of dialogue between them.[2] Moreover, Wilde's first book, *Poems* (1881), was rejected by the Oxford Union after a lively debate about the plagiarisms which it contains.[3] Wilde's tactics have been variously described as borrowings, plagiarism, or self-referentiality; but clearly none of these terms is really adequate, for it is very difficult to attribute a simple motive or simple effect to a device used so frequently and so blatantly. It is not as if Wilde was deceiving an audience or reader, or trying simply to pass off as original work material which was derivative. Moreover, the fact that Wilde borrowed from his own work *and* from that of other writers makes the notion of plagiarism itself complex and difficult to handle. Doubtless, some of the reasons were straightforward and practical. In the years between 1890 and 1894, Wilde was a writer under constant commercial and financial pressure; and so the temptation to be severely economical with his material must have been strong. But it is also true that Wilde enjoyed teasing his audiences, and was clearly aware too that the significance of any 'plagiarized' piece changed profoundly in a new context. How then can Wilde's

[2] So e.g. Act II of *An Ideal Husband* contains material deleted from *A Woman of No Importance* and, in its turn, *The Importance of Being Earnest* contains material from *An Ideal Husband*, also deleted in draft. See *An Ideal Husband*, ed. Russell Jackson, in Wilde, *Two Society Comedies*, ed. Small and Jackson, 199–200.

[3] See Richard Ellmann, *Oscar Wilde* (London, 1987), 140. Ellmann quotes Henry Newbolt's recollections of the debate in *My World as in My Time* (London, 1932), and describes how Oliver Elton called it the work of a 'number of better-known and more deservedly reputed authors. Elton lists, among others, Shakespeare, Sidney, Donne, Byron, Morris, and Swinburne'. (Ellmann, *Oscar Wilde*, 140; Newbolt, *My World*, 96–7.)

compositional tactics be described, and what were their functions?

The central issue in all this is Wilde's engagement with a series of contemporary assumptions about texts, the main one being that an audience reads a text in the expectation of finding qualities such as consistency, originality, and authority. Throughout his *œuvre*, all of these expectations are thwarted in one way or another—and the most striking examples are the apparent inconsistencies in his works. In more of the plays, for example, Wilde reveals a willingness to adapt principles to the needs of a dramatic occasion. A case in point is his inconsistent use of the rules governing social habits such as smoking. In *An Ideal Husband*, a passage was originally drafted in which the sympathetic Lord Goring condones the practice in women. It was later revised to make smoking one of the 'fast' habits of Mrs Cheveley, the play's villainess. In the drafts of the last act of *A Woman of No Importance*, Lord Illingworth is about to take out a cigarette but is rebuked for doing so by Mrs Arbuthnot. In other words, despite Wilde's willingness, as we have seen, to joke about smoking at certain moments in his plays (and in *Dorian Gray*), when the dramatic occasion demanded he was quite happy to make use of the traditional rules regarding women smoking and the impoliteness of smoking in their presence. Similar problems occur with Wilde's use of motifs such as gardens, which at various dramatic moments *within the same play* can denote either innocence or corruption, or on occasions, both.[4] All that remains constant is an audience's

---

[4] The garden motif is used with no consistency at all. At the end of *Lady Windermere's Fan*, the Windermeres escape to an innocence symbolized by the Rose Garden at Selby; in Act IV of *A Woman of No Importance*, Mrs Arbuthnot urges Lord Illingworth to look into the garden of her cottage and witness the innocent love of Hester and Gerald, although we have by then learned that her seduction by Lord Illingworth and 'fall' from innocence took place in her father's garden, and have heard her appeal to him to leave her 'the walled-in garden and the well of water' which her relationship with their illegitimate son represents. (See *A Woman of No Importance*, 68–70.) Early in the play we learn that the 'Book of Life', although it begins 'in a garden', ends 'in Revelations'. (Ibid. 39.) The staging of *A Woman of No Importance* by Herbert Beerbohm Tree in 1893 at the Haymarket emphasized these elements of the play by pointing out by gesture the connections which Wilde makes between 'fallen' sexuality and Nature. (See Russell Jackson and Ian Small, 'Some New Drafts of a Wilde Play', *English Literature in Transition*, 30 (1987), 13.) *The Picture of Dorian Gray* also begins in a garden, and in 'Lord Arthur Savile's Crime', the hero walks through Covent Garden early in the morning. The fullest development of the motif is in the fairy tale 'The Selfish Giant'.

inability to locate with any precision the way in which such motifs are being used on any one occasion.

These observations about Wilde's play with symbols and motifs can also be made about the way the texts operate at a lexical level. It was not unusual for Wilde, as he was composing or revising his work, to delete an adjective or a noun and substitute for it an antonym. The most famous illustration of this occurs with his apparent indecision over the subtitle of *The Importance of Being Earnest: A Trivial Comedy for Serious People.* Through the various drafts which the play underwent, the two adjectives 'trivial' and 'serious' were virtually interchangeable: a trivial comedy for serious people could also mean a serious comedy for trivial people.[5] This interchangeability of a word for its antonym is a constant feature of Wilde's writing, and it is one of the most disconcerting aspects of the genesis of any of his works. Indeed it is possible to construct a set of lexical oppositions which recur throughout the *œuvre* and which Wilde treated as virtually interchangeable: oppositions such as 'moral/immoral'; 'healthy/morbid'; 'serious/trivial'; and so on.[6]

However, these features of Wilde's texts do not operate simply at a lexical level; and neither were the oppositions randomly chosen. Indeed such strategies were deeply subversive of existing categories of thought. Throughout his *œuvre* Wilde wished to redefine the relationship between authority and orthodoxy, and this meant challenging dominant categories of thought. The authority of an orthodoxy (or the social group which utilizes it, an establishment) depends upon the exploitation of these existing categories simply because one of the chief functions of that authority is the production and maintenance of a consensus. Therefore the authority invoked by the iconoclast or the heterodox *must* challenge or overturn those categories simply because his objective has to be the subversion of the consensus of opinion which derives from them. At this point it is worth comparing Wilde's strategies

[5] For details of these particular revisions, see the introduction to Russell Jackson's edition of *The Importance of Being Earnest* (1980; 2nd edn., London, 1988).

[6] See Jonathan Dollimore's immensely suggestive discussion of Wilde's use of binary oppositions and their relationship to what Dollimore calls Wilde's 'transgressive aesthetic' in 'Different Desires: Subjectivity and Transgression in Wilde and Gide', *Textual Practice*, 1 (1987), 48–67.

with those of Pater. Pater appealed to the idea of individuality no less than Wilde did. But Pater's appeal drew upon, or exploited (although, as I have suggested, not in any simple way) existing categories of thought. His strategy invoked an alternative authority which appealed, or looked back, to an older consensus which in the 1870s and 1880s *was in the process of being broken up* by the new forms of scholarship. But Wilde's appeal to the individual, although superficially very similar to that of Pater, was in fact made at a time when that old consensus had been completely dismantled. Hence, unlike Pater, Wilde needed to subvert current categories of thought simply in order to challenge the new consensus which had emerged during Pater's career. Wilde's use of antonyms—his substitution of one term with its opposite—is part of this process of subversion. It was precisely this tactic which Wilde employed as a strategy of argument in *The Soul of Man under Socialism*, where he analyses the contemporary implications of the word 'unhealthy':

The word 'unhealthy', however, admits of analysis. It is a rather interesting word. In fact, it is so interesting that the people who use it do not know what it means. . . . [T]he popular novel that the public call healthy is always a thoroughly unhealthy production; and what the public call an unhealthy novel is always a beautiful and healthy work of art.

I need hardly say that I am not, for a single moment, complaining that the public and the public Press misuse these words. I do not see how, with their lack of comprehension of what Art is, they could possibly use them in the proper sense. I am merely pointing out the misuse; and as for the origin of the misuse and the meaning that lies behind it all, the explanation is very simple. It comes from the barbarous conception of authority. It comes from the natural inability of a community corrupted by authority to understand or appreciate Individualism.[7]

The strategy operating here is also in evidence in Wilde's accounts of the opposition of culture and nature. In the nineteenth century that opposition was deployed to underwrite the idea of representation; in the art criticism of the time a dominant idea, perhaps most powerfully expressed by Ruskin,

[7] Oscar Wilde, *The Soul of Man under Socialism*, in *CW*, 1093–4.

was that pictorial art was successful to the degree to which it either expressed the artist or represented the world of that artist, and in popular art criticism these terms were used with exactly that degree of imprecision. For Wilde, however, the apparently unproblematic relationship between the cultural and the natural was reversed. Wilde challenged this particular orthodoxy by moving to the view that the *cultural* predetermines our expectations or conceptions of the *natural*. His argument was that a culture possesses a codified system of graphic expectations through which and by means of which iconic convention and iconic representation portray our actual knowledge of the real world. This notion is precisely the burden of the most famous lines in 'The Decay of Lying'—Wilde's account of how Impressionist painting of London fogs actually brought about their 'recognition' by his contemporaries:

Where, if not from the Impressionists, do we get those wonderful brown fogs that come creeping down our streets, blurring the gas-lamps and changing the houses into monstrous shadows? To whom, if not to them and their master, do we owe the lovely silver mists that brood over our river, and turn to faint forms of fading grace curved bridge and swaying barge? The extraordinary change that has taken place in the climate of London during the last ten years is entirely due to a particular school of Art. You smile. Consider the matter from a scientific or metaphysical point of view, and you will find that I am right. For what is Nature? Nature is no great mother who has borne us. She is our creation. It is in our brain that she quickens to life. Things are because we see them, and what we see, and how we see it, depends upon the Arts that have influenced us. To look at a thing is very different from seeing a thing. One does not see anything until one sees its beauty. Then, and then only, does it come into existence. . . . There may have been fogs for centuries in London. I dare say there were. But no one saw them, and so we do not know anything about them. They did not exist until Art had invented them.[8]

In Wilde's account art is one of the central ways in which iconic conventions make knowledge about the world possible. In the

<hr>

[8] Wilde, *Intentions*, in *CW*, 986. The term 'nature' is rarely met in his work without the suggestion that any appearance of 'naturalness' is only a contrivance. See the discussion of Hester Worsley's American 'naturalness' in Act II of *A Woman of No Importance* (51): 'MRS ALLONBY. What is that dreadful girl talking about? LADY STUTFIELD. She is painfully natural, is she not?'

years following the publication of *Intentions*, Wilde extended this view to include the spheres of political and social knowledge. For Wilde, the pictorial artefact is also a sign within a larger cultural system of signs, and as such it occupies a place in a system of values which has little or nothing to do with the artefact's artistic or aesthetic values conceived *as* artistic or aesthetic values. Wilde as much as any figure in the nineteenth century knew of the way a man's possessions spoke for him. The Louis Seize cane or furniture, the gold-tipped cigarettes, the carefully selected buttonhole, were possessions that spoke for Wilde and for the central characters in his social dramas. What best announces to the world the taste and values of the clever man are the art-objects which he selects. They locate him very precisely in political and social spheres. In this respect, Wilde's most revealing work is *An Ideal Husband*. In the stage directions for the first act of the first printed edition of the play, Wilde introduces his characters by describing them in terms of their most appropriate portraitists. The artists mentioned are Boucher, Watteau, Lawrence, and Van Dyck. Wilde designates aspects of character by reference to the cultural significance which attaches to the work of specific painters and, by extension, by locating those characters on a social and political (as well as dramatic) spectrum of values. The pictures are not operating as graphic or iconic signs within an aesthetic code, but within other social codes.[9]

Throughout Wilde's critical writing, the sort of strategies

---

[9] The central contrast in *An Ideal Husband* is a political one and is between Van Dyck, the putative portraitist of Sir Robert Chiltern, the play's main character, and Watteau, used to depict two minor female characters of great prettiness and of an 'exquisite fragility'. A typical passage from the stage directions is as follows: '*Sir Robert Chiltern. . . . A personality of mark. Not popular—few personalities are. But intensely admired by the few, and deeply respected by the many. . . . It would be inaccurate to call him picturesque. Picturesqueness cannot survive the House of Commons. But Van Dyck would have loved to paint his head.*' (*An Ideal Husband*, 139–40.) Earlier Mabel Chiltern's modernity is characterized by her being compared to a (recently discovered) Tanagra statuette, and Mrs Cheveley, clearly marked out as a 'fast' and thus socially dangerous woman, is a 'work of art, on the whole, but showing the influence of too many schools' (ibid. 137). A 19th-cent. reading public would quite clearly grasp the distinctions between the established portraitist, connoting order, tradition, and authority, the gentle pastoralism of Watteau, suggestive to the Decadent sensibility of a delicate eroticism, the modernity of a Tanagra statuette, and a style-less eclecticism. The art-objects which Wilde selects themselves implicate the political values which are so central to the play's development.

which he employs in the plays are once more at work, although on a far grander scale. What occurs in miniature at a lexical level becomes in the critical essays a dedicated iconoclasm. Part of that iconoclasm initially has to do with genre. The essays which comprise *Intentions* are usually thought of as literary and art criticism, yet that designation produces (and produced at the time of their publication) more problems than it solves. Wilde's essays, all quite separate and often mutually and self-contradictory, maintain no simple thesis. There is no overriding logic which may be identified as the dominant argument. This is of course part of a consistent and lifelong authorial strategy, exemplified elsewhere in Wilde's deliberate use of devices such as paradox; but it is also part of a very conscious decision to use dialogue as the dominant form in his work. Wilde wished, as it were, to locate his views away from the more usual vehicle for criticism in the 1890s, the periodical or scholarly essay. A clear implication from this decision about genre is that Wilde was anticipating from his contemporary readers a set of responses quite different from those elicited by the writer of the periodical essay. By employing techniques derived from some kinds of drama, Wilde seems to have wanted to produce an argument dependent upon dialectic: to use, that is, one of the specific devices of philosophical dialogue. By the 1890s, as I have indicated in the previous chapter, one of the most usual academic ways of discussing the genre of philosophical dialogue, and in particular the *Dialogues* of Plato, was to stress the effect of the dramatic elements of the texts in question—to see in the speakers in a philosophical dialogue something akin to dramatic characterization. In this view, philosophical argument is not stated: rather, being provisional and unsystematic, it emerges in the course of the dialogue. Clearly Wilde's imitation of such forms—inviting, as it did, comparison with other fictional dialogues, such as W. H. Mallock's *The New Republic* (1877)—had implications for the way in which his works were read. In fact the book did succeed in perplexing its first readers. Despite different opinions about its merits, most reviewers were confused about the seriousness of Wilde's intentions. *The Times* castigated him for a lack of seriousness, for example, and the reviewer in the *Athenaeum* looked forward to criticism from Wilde's pen more like the familiar, reasoned arguments of contemporary critics.[10] This particular line of criticism, though, tended to miss the point, for part of what can be called the generic intention of *Intentions* was that the criteria of relevance and authority which it invoked were of a quite different order from those in the formal critical essays written by Wilde's contemporaries.

Wilde's engagement with authority manifests itself in other ways. At an intellectual level, it translates itself into a reversal of the forms in which critical authority typically presented itself in the work of academics, some of which have been described in earlier chapters. The ambition behind all these forms of iconoclasm was to remove authority in judgements from a consensus of informed individuals—from an academic or scholarly community *and* from journalism—and to restore it to the hands of the individual. Such a view explains what appears at first sight to be mere banter in the dialogue 'The Critic as Artist'. Gilbert and Ernest are discussing classical art criticism:

ERNEST. . . . By the Ilyssus, says Arnold somewhere, there was no Higginbotham. By the Ilyssus, my dear Gilbert, there were no silly art-congresses, bringing provincialism to the provinces and teaching the mediocrity how to mouth. By the Ilyssus there were no tedious magazines about art, in which the industrious prattle of what they do not understand. On the reed-grown banks of that little stream strutted no ridiculous journalism monopolising the seat of judgement when it should be apologising in the dock. The Greeks had no art-critics.

GILBERT. Ernest, you are quite delightful, but your views are terribly unsound. . . . [T]he Greeks were a nation of art-critics, and . . . they invented the criticism of art just as they invented the criticism of everything else.[11]

The Greeks might have invented all forms of intellectual activity, but Wilde's point is that they had no institutions to which and by which those activities were restricted, or, in their turn, no forms of institutional authority which superseded the authority of the individual. And later Gilbert develops his point by insisting that the nature of Greek attitudes to art, particularly those of Aristotle, free as they were from institutional restraints, worked towards the development of the individual:

[10] See *The Times* (7 May 1891), 4; the *Athenaeum* (6 June 1891), 731.
[11] Wilde, *Intentions*, in *CW*, 1015–16.

GILBERT. Concerning himself primarily with the impression that the work of art produces, Aristotle sets himself to analyse that impression, to investigate its source, to see how it is engendered. As a physiologist and psychologist, he knows that the health of a function resides in energy. To have a capacity for passion and not to realise it, is to make oneself incomplete and limited. . . . Tragedy . . . purifies and spiritualises the man.[12]

Wilde's methods at this point actually embody his main argument, in that his texts flout the conventions of measured scholarly debate. There are several obvious ways in which this comes about: the conventions of citation and quotation used to invoke textual and intellectual authority are overturned—the individual becomes his own authority; appeals to collective judgements, which that citation makes possible, are ignored; hence originality and uniqueness of judgement are constantly at a premium; and measured, informed, logical argument is always at a discount.

Citation, as the examples from the plays show, is never a simple matter. Perhaps Wilde's most outrageous flouting of the conventions pertaining to citation occurs in 'Pen, Pencil and Poison'. His principal sources of information were two quite different works on Thomas Wainewright, the poet and poisoner who is the subject of the essay. The first and most obvious source was William Carew Hazlitt's 1880 edition of Waine-wright's *Essays and Criticism* and the biographical essay which Hazlitt included in that edition. The second but much more minor source is Thomas De Quincey's essay 'Charles Lamb'. Wilde's text contains a brief reference to Hazlitt and a conscientious acknowledgement of De Quincey, leading the unwary reader to believe that he has acknowledged his debt to his sources in a manner appropriate to the ways in which they have been used in the text. In fact, his reliance upon Hazlitt is enormous, and on occasions Wilde repeats Hazlitt's essay almost verbatim. Thus Hazlitt:

By one of those chances that are incapable of explanation, a noise in the street attracted his attention, and he pushed aside the blind for a moment to see what it was.[13]

---

[12] Wilde, *Intentions*, in *CW*, 1018.
[13] See William Carew Hazlitt, *Essays and Criticisms of Thomas Griffiths Wainewright* (London, 1880), lxi.

And Wilde, in 'Pen, Pencil and Poison' on the same incident:

It was by a mere accident that he was discovered. A noise in the street attracted his attention, and, in his artistic interest in modern life, he pushed aside the blind for a moment.[14]

Most of the evidence suggests that Wilde wanted to hide this particular source of information, and here his debt is not acknowledged. (An acknowledgement of sorts does occur very near the end of the essay, where Wilde describes himself as being 'indebted' to Hazlitt's book for 'many of the facts' of the essay, and begrudgingly confesses that the work was 'quite invaluable in its way'.[15]) But this is only an extreme example of a systematic strategy to discredit all familiar forms of authority in *Intentions*. As I have indicated, the function of quotation in critical discourse was, by the time Wilde came to write the four pieces which make up *Intentions*, to facilitate the verification and corroboration of source-material. It offered evidence for individual judgements and it made possible the confirmation of that evidence. The function of citation was even more explicit, because it referred the argument of the individual writer to collective judgements of known and tested worth—in other words, to an intellectual orthodoxy. Thus citation in the last decades of the nineteenth century invariably involved reference to authority. Whatever individual abuses there were—such as Matthew Arnold's ambiguous use of authority in some of his critical work—the general corroborative function of citation was well established as a critical practice by 1890.[16]

The two most obvious sources of authority in *Intentions* are Arnold and Pater, but once again Wilde's attitude to both is deeply ambivalent. Arnold is twice invoked in a very obvious way in 'The Critic As Artist':

GILBERT. Yes: it has been said by one whose gracious memory we all revere, and the music of whose pipe once lured Proserpina from her

---

[14] Oscar Wilde, 'Pen, Pencil and Poison', *Intentions*, in *CW*, 1005. The best edition of *Intentions* is by Jacqueline Evans: 'A Critical Edition of Oscar Wilde's *Intentions*' (Ph.D. thesis, Univ. of Birmingham, 1987). I am grateful for Dr Evans for this example of Wilde's plagiarism.

[15] Wilde, *Intentions*, in *CW*, 1007.

[16] For an account of the use of rhetoric and its relationship to authority, see John Holloway, *Victorian Sage* (London, 1953).

Sicilian fields, and made those white feet stir, and not in vain, the Cumnor cowslips, that the proper aim of Criticism is to see the object as in itself it really is. But this is a very serious error, and takes no cognizance of Criticism's most perfect form, which is in its essence purely subjective, and seeks to reveal its own secret and not the secret of another. For the highest Criticism deals with art not as expressive but as impressive purely.[17]

The tone of the passage is revealing, but more important for my argument is the specific character of the reference. The first, to Cumnor's cowslips, is to Arnold as a poet; but the disagreement is with him as a critic; with, that is, Arnold's prescription for objectivity formulated first in 1861 in 'On Translating Homer', but rehearsed in different ways on other occasions in the 1860s.[18] Arnold's general argument is that criticism uniquely provides an atmosphere in which creativity can flourish, and that it should thus embody various intellectual qualities, the most important of which are catholicity, disinterestedness, knowledge, and objectivity.[19] These points are more or less explicitly ignored by Wilde:

Without the critical faculty, there is no artistic creation at all, worthy of the name. You spoke a little while ago of that fine spirit of choice and delicate instinct of selection by which the artist realises life for us, and gives to it a momentary perfection. Well, that spirit of choice, that subtle tact of omission, is really the critical faculty in one of its most characteristic moods, and no one who does not possess this critical faculty can create anything at all in art. Arnold's definition of literature as a criticism of life was not very felicitous in form, but it showed how keenly he recognised the importance of the critical element in all creative work.[20]

In fact on occasions Wilde quite wilfully misreads Arnold. In its context, Arnold's argument is much more modest, and invokes the idea of literature and criticism as forces for a cultural

[17] See Wilde, *Intentions*, in *CW*, 1028.
[18] Arnold's significant re-examination of the phrase, 'to see the object as in itself it really is', occurs in the opening paragraphs of 'The Function of Criticism at the Present Time'. See Matthew Arnold, *Essays in Criticism* (London 1865), 1–41; for elaborations of the points Wilde was concerned with, see esp. ibid. 4–5. Wilde would not have been unaware of the fact that Pater took issue with Arnold's injunction in the preface to *The Renaissance*.
[19] Arnold, 'Function of Criticism', 37–40.
[20] See Wilde, *Intentions*, in *CW*, 1020.

cohesiveness—a condition which, as several critics have noticed, was increasingly less possible as the century progressed and one which Wilde would not in any case have desired.[21] The passage from Arnold's essay which Wilde refers to addresses specifically this social function of criticism:

The critical power is of lower rank than the creative. True; but in assenting to this proposition, one or two things are to be kept in mind. It is undeniable that the exercise of a creative power, that a free creative activity, is the true function of man; it is proved to be so by man's finding in it his true happiness. But it is undeniable, also, that men may have the sense of exercising this free creative activity in other ways than in producing great works of literature or art; if it were not so, all but a very few men would be shut out from the true happiness of all men. They may have it in well-doing, they may have it in learning, they may have it even in criticising.[22]

The significance which attaches to Wilde's use of Arnold is not in the first place to do with the precision with which Arnold's text is used as a source, however, but much more to do with the ambivalence with which Arnold is addressed as an authority. Wilde both invokes 'The Function of Criticism at the Present Time' as an authoritative text, and at the same time challenges the very ground upon which that authority is based. The same general point can be made of Wilde's use of Pater. *The Renaissance* found its way into quite separate works of Wilde. Lord Henry Wotton in *The Picture of Dorian Gray* speaks Pater without fully realizing it—or at least disclosing that he realizes it; and Thomas Wainewright not only speaks the same lines, but shares many aspects of the master's life as well as of his voice:

This young dandy sought to be somebody, rather than do something. . . . He writes about La Gioconda, and early French poets and the Italian Renaissance. He loves . . . Elizabethan translations of *Cupid and Psyche*. . . . He had that curious love of green, which in individuals is always the sign of a subtle artistic temperament, and in

[21] For different views of Wilde's relationship with the dominant forms of 19th-cent. culture, see Raymond Williams, *Culture and Society* (London, 1958); Regenia Gagnier, *Idylls of the Market-Place* (London, 1987); ead., '*De Profundis* as *Epistola: In Carcere et Vinculis*: A Materialist Reading of Oscar Wilde's Autobiography', *Criticism*, 26 (1984), 335–54.
[22] See Matthew Arnold, 'Function of Criticism at the Present Time', 4.

nations is said to denote a laxity, if not a decadence of morals. Like Baudelaire, he was extremely fond of cats, and with Gautier, he was fascinated by that 'sweet marble monster', of both sexes that we can still see at Florence and in the Louvre. . . . In . . . artistic perception he was perfectly right. All beautiful things belong to the same age.[23]

The references here, from the personal (the love of cats and of the colour green) to the literary (to *La Gioconda* and 'Two Early French Stories' in *The Renaissance* and to the Cupid and Psyche narrative in *Marius the Epicurean*) are painstakingly obvious clues, for such a description takes up the stereotyped accounts of Pater which were fairly commonplace in the early 1890s. Later in 'Pen, Pencil and Poison', the identification becomes too obvious:

As an art-critic he concerned himself primarily with the complex impressions produced by a work of art, and certainly the first step in aesthetic criticism is to realise one's own impressions. He cared nothing for abstract discussions on the nature of the Beautiful . . .[24]

Such material, of course, presents the work of Pater and Arnold at a wholly caricatured level. If Pater's work contained a subtle, scholarly, and thus partly disguised interrogation of the authority of critical writing, Wilde's tactics are much more blatant. Citation, reference, and quotation operate as a parody of their accepted functions. Attributed quotations misrepresent arguments; and the use of quotation which is attributed ironically or incorrectly subverts the very authority of quotation, because in the process its validity as argument is controverted. The same basic observation is true of the many minor citations which Wilde uses. *Intentions*, like Pater's work, depends for its effect upon a texture of quotation and reference. 'The Critic As Artist', for example, has scattered references to a plethora of sources. These include classical writers such as Aeschylus, Aristotle, Homer, Longinus, Lucian, Pausanias, Plato, Pliny, Quinctilian, Sophocles, and Virgil; English and American writers such as Augustine Birrell, Browning, Coleridge, Emerson, Henry Arthur Jones, Lewis Morris, Ruskin, William Sharp, Shakespeare, and Tennyson; and European artists, musicians, and writers such as Dante, George Ohnet, L'Abbé

---

[23] See Wilde, *Intentions*, in *CW*, 995–6.

[24] Ibid. 997.

Prévost, Anton Rubinstein, and Wagner. The list is immense, but the main significance of the allusions and references lies not so much in their number, but in the diversity of the familiar and the obscure, the contemporary and the classical: Quinctilian and Aristotle; Ohnet and Dante; Sharp and Shakespeare: the sheer variety is overwhelming. *All* become dignified as authorities; and as such any hierarchy of authority—and indeed the concept of authority itself—is simply lost.

The logic of Wilde's critical practice of course derives from his critical theory. Art for Wilde in *Intentions* is not concerned with imitating the surface phenomena of life but improving upon life by providing a superior model for it. And so art has no use. Its function is to offer a momentary but unreal perfection amid the banal or sordid experiences of life. This reversal of the assumed relationship between the art-object and the world which it represents had one important corollary. Criticism could become analogous with creation, for it was a creative process which could take its material from art instead of from life. By emphasizing the subjectivity of criticism in actively constructing the aesthetic experience, Wilde exonerated the critic from the obligation to say anything about the work of art allegedly under discussion. Indeed, ultimately the critic (like Postlethwaite in Du Maurier's cartoons) was free to draw his material from any source he wished, for he merely took that material as a starting-point for a second creation, namely his own. Indeed, life can in consequence appear as an inferior, and so less satisfying, version of artistic experience. Wilde's logic was that the cultured man should value only the forms and accounts of human experience which could be thus aestheticized. Biography and history—as his essay on Wainewright demonstrates—were to be valued for their 'written' character, for their artefactual elements, rather than for their truth-functions. And in 'The Decay of Lying' pictorial art was to be valued not in the first place for its realism, but for its compositional qualities.

At this juncture it is worth recalling a point which I made in my Introduction, namely that most art and literary criticism associated with the Aesthetic Movement is marked by an absence of discussion of the *art-object* (in the sense defined by Roman Ingarden) and is much more to do with an *aesthetic* object (that is, the art-object as it is subjectively perceived or intersubjectively constructed). The reasons for the appeal of such an aesthetic can now be explained in terms of Wilde's and Pater's challenge to professional authority. Much of the point of professionalization and specialization in the last three decades of the nineteenth century exists precisely in the marking out of specific and exclusive objects of study for each discipline. The deliberate 'failure', or unwillingness, of Wilde or Pater to talk about the object of study of their particular discipline—the art-object—was also a point-blank refusal to be party to the newly specialized academic world. Moreover, as I have suggested, to refuse to be party to the newly specialized academic world was also a refusal to be marginalized. Indeed, one of the consequences of making a claim about the plurality of origins of aesthetic responses was to give to the aesthetic critic a position of pre-eminence, and an unquestioned superiority to the academic critic. His claim was to operate in a world of comprehensive, and thus general, knowledge rather than in a world of specialist, and thus restricted and marginal, knowledge. Wilde's *œuvre* abounds with contemptuous reference to specialist knowledge and celebrations of its opposite; and behind such strategies, it is not difficult to see the distinctions between the general authority of the all-round, accomplished individual (in this case, Wilde himself, of course) and the specious authority of the narrow specialist which Grant Allen had discussed in 'The Decay of Criticism' in the *Fortnightly Review* in 1882.

The consequence of all this was that Wilde, between the years 1889 and 1891, the years, that is, which saw the composition and publication of *Intentions*, was moving to a position from which he could challenge the platitudes and certainties of academic and scholarly discourse. The generic and lexical *jouissance* which I have described are in fact determined by the ideas of subjective responses which 'The Critic as Artist' makes strikingly clear. But related to this notion of subjectivity is a corresponding claim about the plurality of origins of aesthetic responses for the aesthetic critic. As I have indicated, the critic could also draw his material from life—particularly from history. Here the changes in British historiography which I outlined in a previous chapter provided Wilde with immense opportunities. Linda Dowling has suggested that the revolution in historiography had important implications for British *literary* culture, in the sense that it liberated writers from the need to address the relationship between individual moral culpability and historical consequence. Dowling describes in particular the modification of the notion of decline which existed in some earlier Roman historiographies:

The Liberal Anglican interpretation of history thus asserted the intelligibility and hence the moral significance of historical patterns without conceding to those patterns any deterministic coerciveness. In Liberal Anglican texts, historical sequence was moralized and became historical plot. . . . The extensive researches into the Eastern and provincial Empire pursued by Finlay, Mommsen, and such successors as Pelham and J. B. Bury could not be accommodated within [William] Arnold's shapely plot of Roman infancy, adolescence and decline. . . . With the disappearance of Roman decay as the final act of Roman history, the moral significance of Roman decadence disappeared as well. Even historians who were willing for the moment to grant the premise of 'decay' now declined to invest it with the traditional moral explanations.[25]

As a consequence of this, Victorian poets and critics were free to 'aestheticize' the decadence of Rome. The writer was thus able to find in historical sources material whose main interest was not in the first place historical. Historical documents, in a manner not unlike the Aesthetic critic's attitudes to works of art, provided material for creative responses. Dowling describes the perceived amorality of this process:

[I]f Nero is the imperial barbarian who betrays Rome from within it, then Decadent writers themselves, recovering Nero in the name of Art, also represent a betrayal of civilization from within. For the tradition of humane learning that Swinburne, Pater and [Lionel] Johnson represent has, in their recuperation of Nero as the playful artist of torture, the great master of death and lust, been turned against humane ends. Or at least so most Victorians would have said.[26]

This freedom to aestheticize rather than moralize history becomes in *Intentions* part of the critic's larger freedom to dispute and to disown authority. In 'Pen, Pencil and Poison' Wilde

[25] Linda Dowling, 'Roman Decadence and Victorian Historiography', *Victorian Studies*, 28 (1985), 587, 599.
[26] Ead., 'Nero and the Aesthetics of Torture', *Victorian Newsletter*, 66 (1984), 5.

refers to his new-found ability to treat of historical personages as characters of aesthetic rather than moral or historical interest. They become, that is, analogous to dramatic creations:

I know that there are many historians, or at least writers on historical subjects, who still think it necessary to apply moral judgments to history, and who distribute their praise or blame with the solemn complacency of a successful schoolmaster. This, however, is a foolish habit, and merely shows that the moral instinct can be brought to such a pitch of perfection that it will make its appearance wherever it is not required. Nobody with the true historical sense ever dreams of blaming Nero, or scolding Tiberius, or censuring Caesar Borgia. These personages have become like the puppets of a play. They may fill us with terror, or horror, or wonder, but they do not harm us. They are not in immediate relation to us. We have nothing to fear from them. They have passed into the sphere of art and science, and neither art nor science knows anything of moral approval or disapproval. And so it may be some day with Charles Lamb's friend.[27]

Wilde uses, that is, an historiographical strategy in order to remove Wainewright's life from the domain of moral judgement and to assert once more his freedom from the constraints that usually operated on academic or scholarly discourse.

In all these ways—the abuse of scholarly apparatus and procedure, citation, and quotation; the use of antonyms to subvert existing categories of thought and to disable the existing practices of art and literary criticism; the fictionalizing of historical discourse and the consequent destruction of the unique authority of that discourse to deal in 'truth' and in 'facts'—Wilde challenged the relationship between authority and institutional orthodoxy, and thus challenged the traditional relationships between authority and knowledge. Wilde thus redefines authority and places it in the hands of the man of taste—the Aesthete, the exemplar of whom was of course Wilde himself. The final paradox of Wilde was to present himself at one and the same time as an enemy of authority *and* as a great teacher, unstinting with his advice on art and life, but insisting (in the words he gives to Lord Goring, the Aesthete–hero of *An Ideal Husband*) that the only thing to do with good advice is to pass it on—'It is never of any use to oneself'.[28]

[27] Wilde, *Intentions*, in *CW*, 1008.
[28] Id., *An Ideal Husband*, 167.

6

Conclusion:
Knowledge and Authority

The objective of this book has been twofold: first to describe the forms of a general intellectual crisis of authority in the last third of the nineteenth century and the implications of it; and secondly, to explain the work of Pater and Wilde in terms of that crisis. From such an account several different kinds of conclusions may now be drawn.

The first kind of conclusion is one specific to the interpretation of Pater and Wilde. There has been a longstanding tendency among literary historians to see late nineteenth-century writers as marginal. In fact this tendency began in the 1890s and persisted in one form or another until the 1940s and 1950s when it was given added emphasis by such influential critics as F. W. Bateson and F. R. Leavis.[1] Fashions have changed somewhat in recent years, but the dominant view of the late nineteenth century among literary critics is still one which tends to deny or ignore the uniqueness of writers such as Pater and Wilde, and stresses instead their anticipation of the early modernists who succeeded them. It is still taken for granted that Wilde and Pater worked in a rarified atmosphere, an environment far removed from the major academic and intellectual concerns of their time. However, the ideational context in which this book has attempted to place both of them suggests that this view is simply a misguided one and that they should instead be considered as serious figures in that they obviously did engage with dominant intellectual issues.

There is, moreover, another dimension to this particular

---

[1] See F. W. Bateson (ed.), *Cambridge Bibliography of English Literature*, iii (Cambridge, 1940), where Pater is identified as a 'critic and miscellaneous writer', and Wilde is seen principally as a dramatist. F. R. Leavis's criticism is significant because of its failure to discuss virtually all writers of the 1880s and 1890s.

contextualization of Pater and Wilde, for it enables the historian to account for the relationship between the life and the work of both in terms other than just that of homosexuality, but in a way which is not incompatible with it. As I have indicated in my account of Pater, some recent critics have sought to define authority in terms of power and gender.[2] While these and other accounts have made interesting suggestions about the nature of, and relationship between, power and gender, the analyses which they present are somewhat limited in the senses that power and gender are not, as these writers tend to assume, in themselves isolated social phenomena. Accounts of power and gender, particularly as they relate to forms of intellectual activity, must logically be preceded by a discussion of the relationship between knowledge and authority, precisely because notions of power and gender have little meaning beyond the institutions which sanction them, and these sanctions may in their turn only be understood in terms of the operation of intellectual authority in institutions.

The most significant claim to be made on behalf of this relocation of Pater and Wilde is that it generates interesting and radical interpretations both of their work *and* of their lives as writers. Some recent studies have attempted to appropriate Pater and Wilde specifically on the grounds that they are radical writers.[3] But 'radicalism' in these cases is defined in a particularly narrow way: it is understood to apply to work which has relevant and timely implications for issues in contemporary British society. In fact, it is not necessary to resort to strategies such as these in order to argue the case for either Pater's or Wilde's radicalism. As the argument of this book has suggested, to look both at the questions with which Wilde and Pater were concerned during their lives, and at the variety of answers which they proposed, not only demonstrates their radicalism at the time, but also demonstrates the relevance of that radicalism to modern debates. Or to put the argument in its most general terms: past writers can indeed be relevant to

[2] See Thomas Docherty, *On Modern Authority: The Conditions of Writing from 1100 to the Present* (Brighton, 1987); and Ed Cohen, 'Writing gone Wilde: Homoerotic Desire in the Closet of Representation', *PMLA*, 102 (1987), 801–13.

[3] See esp. Jonathan Dollimore, 'Different Desires: Subjectivity and Transgression in Wilde and Gide', *Textual Practice*, 1 (1987), 48–67.

contemporary issues and to contemporary debates about those issues, but the grounds of that relevance have to be determined by *their* concerns, and not by *ours*.

This point in itself leads directly to a second kind of conclusion—and it is the more important one because it has the widest and most controversial implications. The particularities and details of the intellectual crisis which I have described are of course unique to the nineteenth century, but the fundamental structure of the crisis—the relationship between authority and knowledge—is not. An awareness of this structure has important implications for the various intellectual dilemmas of the present day, particularly for the contemporary 'crisis in English' so often alluded to in recent academic literary journals. And if indeed there are these structural similarities, then the methodology which has been employed in this study can be used to investigate the nature of the current crisis. In the first place, an understanding of the structure of the nineteenth-century crisis allows a precise characterization of its latter-day counterpart. The purpose of this book was to describe the crisis in the late nineteenth century in *intellectual* rather than in institutional terms, a characterization equally applicable to the present dilemma in English studies. Most critics have tended to describe the current crisis in institutional terms,[4] but the fact that there is a wide divergence of opinion within English about what is to count as an appropriate theory of literary studies suggests that the nature of the contemporary crisis is also fundamentally intellectual, and hence the reasons for its occurrence will be the same as any intellectual crisis, including my nineteenth-century example, namely those of intellectual authority and epistemology.

As I have indicated, a crisis in intellectual authority is always caused by competition between the epistemologies which underwrite that authority. This pattern of events has recurred in English departments in the last two decades. From about 1970 onwards, new and competing epistemologies precipitated a series of crises in the nature of intellectual authority in some humanities disciplines. The object of study in English, like

---

[4] See e.g. Terence Hawkes, 'Editorial', *Textual Practice*, 1 (1987); Terry Eagleton, 'End of English', *Textual Practice*, 1 (1987), 1–9; Peter Widdowson, 'Terrorism and Literary Studies', *Textual Practice*, 2 (1988), 1–21.

some other humanities disciplines, might well be different in nature from the objects of study of other disciplines of knowledge, but the structure of the relationship between its epistemology and intellectual authority is identical. A single discipline cannot tolerate *competing* epistemologies, although it may tolerate differing epistemologies which are *not* in competition; however, it can tolerate competing methodologies. Hence, for example, the discipline of history, where competing methodologies coexist, has *not* experienced a similar sense of crisis as the one which obtains in English today. In a programmatic form, then, the current intellectual crisis in English can be stated very briefly. Authority became the central issue for English studies after about 1970 because several different epistemologies were being used to underwrite that authority, and these epistemologies were in competition with each other.

The situation at present is that, as in some disciplines of knowledge in the 1870s and 1880s, competing critical theories invoke vastly different epistemologies to validate their critical practices and therefore to validate what is to count as explanation within those theories. Thus, to reiterate some of the examples given in the Introduction, structuralism has used a linguistic model of human activity, a concept of humans as sign-making animals. Feminist criticism, on the other hand, has tended (although not exhaustively so) to look to psychology for an epistemology, and in this epistemology the 'human' is characterized in terms of desires, wishes, and so forth. And, as I have suggested earlier, Marxist criticism depends upon an 'economic' model of human activity to validate its practices and observations. In this respect, matters are further complicated by the fact that some critical theories are applications or aspects of larger, more systematically theorized philosophies, while others employ more than one epistemology. Certain feminist critiques, for example, combine linguistic and Freudian, or Marxist and Freudian, epistemologies. Each of the examples given above demonstrates that contemporary criticism has derived its principles of validation and therefore its intellectual authority from the epistemologies of other disciplines of knowledge. But, as in the nineteenth-century example, they are not simply different explanations; they are different *sorts* of explanation. Concepts of literary meaning, therefore, despite whatever local agreements or disagreements there might be, are not only derived from different origins, but are of quite different natures.

These observations in their turn point to the reason why the debate over theory, once again like its nineteenth-century counterpart, has been marked by bitter disagreement and why it has been fruitless in the sense that few, if any, of the issues raised by it have yet been resolved. One theory may, on the grounds outlined above, be right, but it has no way of proving rival theories wrong or incorrect. For a theory to rebut or refute contending theories, that is, there has to be a common epistemology, or at least the conditions for an agreement about epistemology. The possibility of correctness or incorrectness depends upon the grounds of falsifiability or verifiability being established beforehand, and hence upon further agreement about what is to count as evidence, argument, and so forth. Given that there is, in contemporary critical debate, no such agreement, no one theory can refute or rebut any other. It can merely reject it or discount it. The consequence is that what is erroneously labelled theoretical debate is in fact the clash of dogmas, in which nothing can be agreed and nothing can be refuted, because there are no grounds for agreement or refutation. And the logic of that situation is that either English as a discipline will exist in a state of continuing crisis, or, as in the late nineteenth century, a dominant epistemology, and therefore a dominant intellectual authority, will begin to re-emerge.

The second set of general implications which may be drawn from my account of the late nineteenth-century intellectual crisis concerns the relationship between the practice labelled 'literary criticism' and the determination of literary values. The nineteenth-century crisis, as I have outlined, occurred precisely at the moment when 'English' was being institutionalized and professionalized in the universities. As I have indicated in my Introduction, common to all nascent professions is an attempt to delimit, and then lay exclusive claim to, a particular practice. The grounds of those decisions about delimitation and appropriation are that the practice in question should possess a valuable, because unique, kind of knowledge. And that knowledge in its turn is restricted to those who have been specially trained in the methods of that exclusive practice—in other words, knowledge becomes restricted to 'professionals'. Now, in the case of English, that practice was of course literary criticism. Algernon Moncrieff's banter with Jack Worthing in the first act of *The Importance of Being Earnest* ('Literary criticism is not your forte my dear fellow. Don't try it. You should leave that to people who haven't been at a University')[5] is only dramatically effective because by 1895 precisely the opposite situation obtained. Prior to the 1870s, there were various ways of talking about 'texts' (to use as neutral a term as possible) —in, for example, reviewing, or in *belles-lettres*, or in biography, and so forth. But there was no specialized body of knowledge which restricted these practices to specific texts. Moreover, there were no specialist practitioners: there were no professional critics in the senses in which I have defined 'professional'. Indeed all of the great Victorian 'sages' had other careers. Nor at this time was there any dissent or confusion over the idea of 'literariness'—recall, for example, John Stuart Mill's characterization of literary qualities which makes no distinction between *kinds or classes* of texts. So texts by authors as diverse as Spinoza, Shakespeare, Adam Smith, Walter Scott, and Macaulay could be described by figures as varied as Thomas Carlyle, Matthew Arnold, and Grant Allen as possessing literary qualities. The term 'literary', that is, was not used to indicate or to mark off a particular category of works in the way that it tends to do today. However, in the 1870s and 80s, again as I have suggested, the process of professionalization did not proceed unchallenged. Wilde's and Pater's prescriptions for Aesthetic criticism were attempts to provide an alternative definition for the practice of literary criticism; and, following from this, an attempt to define also an alternative kind of knowledge which that practice could produce.

Now this conflict between, on the one hand, the prescriptions for literary criticism produced within the universities, and on the other, those produced by writers such as Wilde and Pater, was manifest most clearly in a debate about the nature of *literary value*, for notoriously Wilde and Pater were seen to be denying that literature could embody any *moral value*. The nature of that debate has been documented elsewhere,[6] but the important

[5] Wilde, *The Importance of Being Earnest*, ed. Russell Jackson (1980; 2nd edn., London, 1988), 14.
[6] See e.g. the treatment of the topic in R. V. Johnson, *Aestheticism* (London, 1969).

point to notice here is that literary value only became contested when the nature of literary criticism was itself in dispute. Logically this observation suggests that the notion of literariness is inseparable from the practice of literary criticism; or rather, as the 'literary' becomes the object of study of the discipline of literary criticism, so literary criticism tends to monopolize definitions of the 'literary'. Generally speaking, the concept of the 'literary' which marks off a particular *category of texts* from all other texts needs to—and perhaps can—exist only when a particular practice—literary criticism—has to lay claim to specialist knowledge. (This process occurs, of course, simply because the status and value of specialist knowledge lies precisely in the fact that it must be restricted.) Such a situation explains exactly why Pater's and Wilde's opposition to the professionalization of English within the universities took the form of offering a theory and a programme of critical practice which did *not* limit itself to particular texts, and hence an aesthetic programme which did not limit itself to works of art. To do otherwise was to mimic the practices of the newly professionalized literary critics, and therefore accept as legitimate both their claim to a specialist knowledge, and their right to appoint special guardians of that knowledge. For also in Pater's and Wilde's proposals, as I have argued above, was the claim that the necessary qualifications to practise literary criticism required no specialist qualifications or training, for it resided within, and was innate to, the individual. It was not, that is, a quality which could be described in specific terms, such as a skill; and, more importantly, neither could it ever be taught, measured or examined by any external body. It was innate to the psychology of the individual. It was Pater's and Wilde's uniqueness which qualified them to practise literary criticism; and uniqueness, in their view residing in the individual sensibility, is possessed by all.

I am now in a position to offer some final general points. The institutional constraints which placed restrictions on the texts deemed to be 'literary' enabled the teaching and study of literature to be given specific *social* functions. Such a situation was, of course, exactly what was to be expected; for one of the criteria for professionalization, as I have outlined in my Introduction, was that the knowledge possessed by any profession, if not socially necessary, needed at the very least to demonstrate a form of social utility. As in law, medicine, engineering, and so forth, literary criticism as a professional activity had to serve the general public. The most general way in which this could be done was to argue that literature could first embody, and then transmit, what were then perceived as essential moral values. Now this idea was of course not new; it had existed in one form or other since antiquity and had been commonplace, as I have also indicated, in the early part of the nineteenth century. But if the idea itself was not new, the particular ways in which it was institutionalized most certainly were.

The first of these ways was a reinforcing of classical by vernacular literature for the teaching of what contemporary pedagogy chose to call civilized values. And in this respect it is worth recalling that 'English' became an important component in the new Civil Service examinations in the middle decades of the century: gentlemanly and civilized qualities were those deemed appropriate for civil or government service in India. (Wilde again was to have his view on this: in Act III of *A Woman of No Importance*, Lord Illingworth advises his son Gerald Arbuthnot that 'examinations are of no value whatsoever. If a man is a gentleman, he knows quite enough, and if he is not a gentleman, whatever he knows is bad for him.'[7]) To bring 'English values' to colonial India involved the teaching of English to the purveyors of those values. And this idea was extended to include the proposal of a national literature. Here it was argued that a special group of works—a canon—was capable of serving national interests in so far as they embodied and preserved what was essential to 'Englishness'.[8] There are numerous examples of this process, but for my argument one will be sufficient. In 1880 T. H. Ward was commissioned to produce a set of texts for schools entitled *English Poets*, and each poet was to be introduced by an eminent critic. The function which the series was intended to fulfil is perhaps best described by John Campbell Shairp in his review of the first volume in the

---

[7] Oscar Wilde, *A Woman of No Importance*, ed. Ian Small, in Oscar Wilde, *Two Society Comedies*, ed. Ian Small and Russell Jackson (London, 1983), 73.

[8] On this point, see Linda Dowling, *Language and Decadence in the Victorian Fin de Siècle* (Princeton, NJ, 1986), who argues that the concept of a specifically 'national' literature was an answer to a crisis in imperialism; and Robert Colls and Philip Dodd (ed.), *Englishness* (London, 1986).

Quarterly Review in 1882; it was one clearly associated with definitions of Englishness and the 'English' character:

The poetry of England is the bloom of her national life. It contains the essence, expressed in the most beautiful form, of whatever is highest and deepest, most vivid and most pathetic, in the thoughts and sentiments which have swayed our countrymen during the successive ages of their history. . . . The roll of English poetry, reaching through 500 years, contains the essence of the national life—it registers the pulsations of the mighty heart of England during all those centuries. It mirrors whatever is best and brightest, if also what is most mournful and pathetic, in the experience of our countrymen. But the roll, we trust, is not yet filled up. Unless the heart of our people has lost its ancient power, its future throbbings will yet be heard in a new and invigorated poetry, which shall be worthy of the language that Chaucer formed and Shakespeare spoke.[9]

Shairp was a particularly appropriate choice for reviewer in that he was one of the most conspicuous of the newly professionalized and newly institutionalized literary critics. In June 1877 he had succeeded Sir Francis Charles Doyle as Professor of Poetry at Oxford, and he was reappointed in 1882. The substance of the twelve lectures (published in 1881) which Shairp delivered during his tenure of that chair at Oxford was a fierce indictment of the critical practices of Aestheticism. Condemnation such as this was, of course, precisely the revenge enacted upon figures such as Pater and Wilde by British academic institutions. To his contemporaries Pater was never a serious 'scholar' and the allegations about his misquotations have persisted to the present day.[10] And in his own lifetime Wilde, as I have shown, although he was often regarded as clever or brilliant, was also never considered a serious writer.

The point to be emphasized is that these and other pedagogic and national claims being made for 'English' depended in the first place upon the prior professionalization and institutionalization of literary criticism. This process had delivered 'Literature' into the hands of professional specialists, and so allowed

---

[9] John Campbell Shairp, 'English Poets and Oxford Critics', *Quarterly Review*, 153 (1882), 431, 463.

[10] This general line of argument runs through an essay as recent as that by Christopher Ricks, 'Arnold, Pater and Misquotation', *TLS*, 3948 (25 Nov. 1977), 1383–5.

that group of specialists several powers. The first was to determine what was common to all 'Literature'; secondly, to decide what specialist knowledge was appropriate to it and what values were endorsed by it; and thirdly to control, through their authority as the only qualified practitioners of that profession, the dissemination of this knowledge and these values.

Once the criteria for 'literariness' had been constrained by professional academic criticism to the notion of a class of texts, then the practice of literary criticism was free to decide what members were to be included in that class. The most fundamental of these decisions concerned the positing of a particular style—to use Shairp's term in 1882, the 'noble English style'—which texts, in order to be designated as literary, or as 'Literature', had to display. Interestingly these stylistic prescriptions were not confined to linguistic, nor indeed to formal, qualities. They included such attributes as 'manliness', 'freshness', 'health', and so forth. So the process of defining the category of literature typically set up the following oppositions: 'serious/trivial'; 'professional/amateur'; 'manly/effeminate'; 'healthy/sick'. It is worth reiterating that Pater and Wilde were always placed in the subordinate positions of these hierarchies. Typically they were characterized as 'unhealthy' and 'effeminate' or 'unmanly'; indeed Rossetti (who was half-Italian) and Wilde (who was Irish) were specifically 'un-English'. Thus these writers were invariably placed outside the domain of 'true literature', in as far as it was defined by the professional literary critics. (This is not to say, of course, that contemporaries, such as W. B. Yeats or George Moore accepted such categorizations: indeed they claimed, but on other grounds, literary qualities in the work of all three.) Such a situation has another set of implications: that the criteria proposed by institutionalized literary criticism were conceived as a strategy to exclude certain writers as well as to include others. It is also true to say that as literary criticism changed its objectives, so too it modified the criteria for its category of 'literariness', and thus changed or extended the range of texts it wished to include in that category. Such decisions were not of course arbitrary; but neither were they permanent or 'essential'. They would last, and remain valid, for as long—but only for as long—as the institutional practice which endorsed them retained its status.

These observations, if they are correct, have some very clear implications for the present time: defining the relationship between the practices of literary criticism and the determination of literary value in the way I have attempted in this book makes it possible to understand and reassess contemporary disputes over the notion of literary value itself, and over critical practices. These debates have exhibited a considerable rancour, especially in the dispute over 'the canon' of literary texts to be taught in institutions of higher education and in the analagous dispute over the range of artistic forms—such as popular fiction, film studies, and the literatures of nationalities other than British—which contemporary literary criticism should address. In all these disputes, the *structure* of the contemporary crisis over knowledge and authority in literary criticism is identical to that of its nineteenth-century predecessor.

Select Bibliography

ABBOTT, ANDREW, 'Status and Strain in the Professions', *American Journal of Sociology*, 86 (1981), 819–35.

ABBOTT, EVELYN (ed.), *Hellenica* (London, 1880).

ABRAMS, PHILIP, *The Origins of British Sociology* (Chicago, Ill., 1968).

ADAM, J. (ed.), *The Apology of Plato* (London, 1888).

—— *The Crito of Plato* (London, 1888).

—— *The Republic of Plato* (London, 1897).

ADELMAN, PAUL, 'Frederic Harrison and the "Positivist" Attack on Orthodox Political Economy', *History of Political Economy*, 3 (1971), 170–89.

ALISON, ARCHIBALD, *Essay on the Nature and Principles of Taste* (Edinburgh, 1790).

ALLEN, GRANT, *Physiological Aesthetics* (London, 1877).

—— 'Decay of Criticism', *Fortnightly Review*, 37 (1882), 339–51.

—— 'Aesthetic Evolution in Man', *Mind*, 5 (1880), 445–64.

ARNOLD, MATTHEW, *Essays in Criticism* (London, 1865).

—— *Culture and Anarchy* (London, 1869).

BAGEHOT, WALTER, *Economic Studies*, ed. R. Holt Hutton (1879; 2nd edn., London, 1880).

BAIN, ALEXANDER, 'Mr James Ward's "Psychology"', *Mind*, 11 (1886), 457–77.

—— 'On "Association" Controversies', *Mind*, 12 (1887), 161–82.

—— *The Senses and the Intellect* (London, 1855).

—— *The Emotions and the Will* (1859; 2nd edn., London, 1865).

—— *Mental and Moral Science* (London, 1868–72).

BALDICK, CHRIS, *The Social Mission of English Criticism 1848–1932* (Oxford, 1983).

BANN, STEPHEN, *The Clothing of Clio: A Study of the Representation of History in Nineteenth-Century Britain and France* (Cambridge, 1984).

BARBER, BERNARD, 'Some Problems in the Sociology of Professions', *Daedalus*, 92 (1963), 669–88.

BAUMGARTEN, ALEXANDER, *Aesthetica* (Frankfurt-on-Oder, 1750–8).

BEN-ISRAEL, HEDVA, *Historians on the French Revolution* (Cambridge, 1968).

BENN, A. W., *The Greek Philosophers* (2 vols., London, 1880).

BIRKEN, LAWRENCE, 'From Macroeconomics to Microeconomics: The Marginalist Revolution in Sociocultural Perspective', *History of Political Economy*, 20 (1988), 251–64.

BIZOT, RICHARD, 'Pater in Transition', *Philological Quarterly*, 52 (1973), 129–41.

BLACK, R. D. COLLISON, 'W. S. Jevons and the Foundation of Modern Economics', *History of Political Economy*, 4 (1972), 364–78.

—— 'The Papers and Correspondence of William Stanley Jevons: A Supplementary Note', *Manchester School*, 50 (1982), 417–28.

—— COATS, A. W., and GOODWIN, CRAUFURD D. W. (eds.), *The Marginal Revolution in Economics: Interpretation and Evaluation* (Durham, NC, 1973).

BOCK, KENNETH, *The Acceptance of Histories* (Berkeley, Calif., 1956).

BOSANQUET, BERNARD, *A Companion to Plato's Republic* (London, 1895).

—— *A History of Aesthetic* (London, 1892).

BRAKE, LAUREL, and SMALL, IAN (eds.), *Walter Pater in the 1990s* (Greensboro, NC, forthcoming, 1991).

BREISACH, ERNST, *Historiography: Ancient, Medieval and Modern* (Chicago, Ill., 1983).

BUCKLE, HENRY, *History of Civilization in England* (1857–61; London, 1872).

BURROW, J. W., *Evolution and Society* (Cambridge, 1966).

—— *A Liberal Descent: Victorians and the English Past* (Cambridge, 1981).

BYWATER, INGRAM (ed.), *Heracliti Ephesii Reliquiae* (Oxford, 1877).

CAMPBELL, LEWIS (ed.), *The Theatetus of Plato* (1861; London, 1882).

CAPES, W. W., *Stoicism* (London, 1880).

CARLYLE, THOMAS, *Past and Present* (London, 1843).

CARO, E., 'La Critique contemporaine et les causes de son affaiblissement', *Revue des deux mondes*, 49 (1882), 547–66.

CHARLTON, H. B., *Portrait of A University 1851–1951* (Manchester, 1951).

CHARTERIS, EVAN, *The Life and Letters of Sir Edmund Gosse* (London, 1931).

CHECKLAND, S. G., 'Economic Opinion in England as Jevons found It', *Manchester School*, 2 (1951), 143–69.

COATS, A. W., 'Sociological Aspects of British Economic Thought (ca. 1880–1930)', *Journal of Political Economy*, 75 (1967), 706–25.

—— 'The Role of Authority in the Development of British Economics', *Journal of Law and Economics*, 7 (1964) 85–106.

COHEN, ED, 'Writing gone Wilde: Homoerotic Desire in the Closet of Representation', *PMLA*, 102 (1897), 801–13.

COLLINI, STEFAN, WINCH, DONALD, and BURROW, JOHN, *That Noble Science of Politics: A Study in Nineteenth-Century Intellectual History* (Cambridge, 1983).

COLLINS, JOHN CHURTON, 'English Literature at the Universities', *Quarterly Review*, 163 (1886), 289–339.

COLLS, ROBERT, and DODD, PHILIP(eds.), *Englishness* (London, 1986).

COOK, A. B., *The Metaphysical Basis of Plato's Ethics* (Cambridge, 1895).

DAVIES, J. LLEWELYN, and VAUGHAN, D. J. (eds.), *The Republic of Plato* (2nd edn., London, 1886).

DELLAMORA, RICHARD, 'Representation and Homophobia in *The Picture of Dorian Gray*', *Victorian Newsletter*, 73 (1988), 28–31.

DEMARCHI, N. B., 'The Noxious Influence of Authority: A Correction of Jevons's Charge', *Journal of Law and Economics*, 16 (1973), 179–89.

DESSAU, HERMANN, 'Über Zeit und Persönlichkeit der S.H.A.', *Hermes*, 24 (1889), 337–92.

—— 'Über die S.H.A.', *Hermes* 27 (1892), 561–605.

DOCHERTY, THOMAS, *On Modern Authority: The Conditions of Writing from 1100 to the Present* (Brighton, 1987).

DODD, PHILIP (ed.), *Walter Pater: An Imaginative Sense of Fact* (London, 1981).

DOLLIMORE, JONATHAN, 'Different Desires: Subjectivity and Transgression in Wilde and Gide', *Textual Practice*, 1 (1987), 48–67.

DOWLING, LINDA, 'Nero and the Aesthetics of Torture', *Victorian Newsletter*, 66 (1984), 1–5.

—— 'Roman Decadence and Victorian Historiography', *Victorian Studies*, 28 (1985), 579–605.

—— *Language and Decadence in the Victorian Fin de Siècle* (Princeton, NJ, 1986).

EAGLETON, TERRY, 'The End of English', *Textual Practice*, 1 (1987), 1–9.

EKELUND, ROBERT B. jun., and HÉBERT, ROBERT F., *A History of Economic Theory and Method* (1975; 2nd edn., New York, 1983).

ELLIOT, PHILIP, *The Sociology of the Professions* (London, 1962).

ELLMANN, RICHARD, *Oscar Wilde* (London, 1987).

EVANS, JACQUELINE W., 'A Critical Edition of Oscar Wilde's "Intentions"' (Ph.D. thesis, Univ. of Birmingham, 1987).

EVANS, LAWRENCE (ed.), *The Letters of Walter Pater* (Oxford, 1970).

FELPERIN, HOWARD, 'Making it "Neo": The New Historicism and Renaissance Literature', *Textual Practice*, 1 (1987), 262–77.

FISHER, ROBERT M., *The Logic of Economic Discovery: Neoclassical Economics and the Marginal Revolution* (Brighton, 1986).

FLETCHER, IAN, *Walter Pater* (London, 1959).

FOUCAULT, MICHEL, *The Order of Things* (London, 1970).

—— *The Archeology of Knowledge*, tr. A. M. Sheridan Smith (London, 1972).

GAGNIER, REGENIA, '*De Profundis* as *Epistola: In Carcere et Vinculis*: A Materialist Reading of Oscar Wilde's Autobiography', *Criticism*, 26 (1984), 335–54.

—— *The Idylls of the Market-Place* (Aldershot, 1987).

GAUNT, WILLIAM, *The Aesthetic Adventure* (revd. edn., London, 1975).

GEERTZ, CLIFFORD, *The Interpretation of Cultures* (London, 1975).

GOLDSTEIN, DORIS, 'The Professionalization of History in the Late Nineteenth and Early Twentieth Centuries', *Storia della storiografia*, 1 (1983), 3–23.

GOOCH, G. P., *History and Historians* (London, 1952).

GOODE, WILLIAM J., 'Community within a Community: The Professions', *American Sociological Review*, 22 (1957), 194–200.

GOSSE, EDMUND, *From Shakespeare to Pope: An Enquiry into the Causes and Phenomena of the Rise of Classical Poetry in England* (Cambridge, 1885).

GROSSKURTH, PHYLLIS, 'Churton Collins: Scourge of the Late Victorians', *University of Toronto Quarterly*, 34 (1965), 254–68.

HALSEY, A. H., and TROW, M. A., *The British Academics* (London, 1971).

HARTLEY, DAVID, *Observations on Man, his Frame, his Duty and his Expectations* (London, 1749).

HARVIE, CHRISTOPHER, *The Lights of Liberalism: University Liberals and the Challenge of Democracy 1860–1886* (London, 1976).

HAWTHORN, GEOFFREY, *Enlightenment and Despair: A History of Social Theory* (1976; 2nd edn., Cambridge, 1987).

HAZLITT, WILLIAM CAREW, *Essays and Criticisms of Thomas Griffiths Wainewright* (London, 1880).

HEYCK, T. W., *The Transformation of Intellectual Life in Victorian England* (London, 1982).

HOLLOWAY, JOHN, *The Victorian Sage* (London, 1953).

HOSPERS, JOHN (ed.), *Introductory Readings in Aesthetics* (New York, 1969).

HOUGH, GRAHAM, *The Last Romantics* (London, 1949).

HUGHES, EVERETT, 'Professions', *Daedalus*, 92 (1963), 655–67.

HUNT, E. K., *History of Economic Thought: A Critical Perspective* (Belmont, Calif., 1979).

HUTCHISON, T. W., *A Review of Economic Doctrines 1870–1929* (Westport, Conn., 1975).

—— *On Revolutions and Progress in Economic Knowledge* (Cambridge, 1978).

—— 'The Politics and Philosophy in Jevons's Political Economy', *Manchester School*, 50 (1982), 366–78.

HUXLEY, THOMAS, 'The Scientific Aspects of Positivism', *Fortnightly Review*, 11 (1869), 653–70.

INGARDEN, ROMAN, 'Artistic and Aesthetic Values', in *Aesthetics*, ed. Harold Osborne (1972; Oxford, 1978), 39–54.

JACKSON, J. A. (ed.), *Professions and Professionalization* (Cambridge, 1970).

JACKSON, RUSSELL, and SMALL, IAN, 'Some New Drafts of a Wilde Play', *English Literature in Transition*, 30 (1987), 7–15.

JEVONS, WILLIAM STANLEY, *Letters and Journals of William Stanley Jevons* (ed.) H. A. Jevons (London, 1886).

—— *Theory of Political Economy* (1871; London, 1957).

JOHNSON, R. V., *Aestheticism* (London, 1969).

JONES, ERNEST, *Hamlet and Oedipus* (London, 1949).

KEARNEY, ANTHONY, *John Churton Collins: The Louse on the Locks of Literature* (Edinburgh, 1985).

KENT, CHRISTOPHER, *Brains and Numbers: Elitism, Comtism and Democracy in Mid-Victorian Britain* (Toronto, 1978).

KEYNES, JOHN MAYNARD, 'William Stanley Jevons 1835–1882: A Centenary Allocution on his Life as Economist and Statistician', *Journal of the Royal Statistical Society*, 99 (1936), 516–48.

KINGDON, G. T., *An Essay on the Protagoras of Plato* (Cambridge, 1875).

KLEIN, D. B., *A History of Scientific Psychology* (London, 1970).

KNIGHT, WILLIAM, *The Philosophy of the Beautiful* (2 vols., London, 1891).

KOOT, GERARD M., 'English Historical Economics and the Emergence of Economic History in England', *History of Political Economy*, 12 (1980), 174–205.

KRISTELLER, PAUL OSKAR, 'The Modern System of the Arts: A Study in the History of Aesthetics: (I)', *Journal of the History of Ideas*, 12 (1951), 496–527.

—— 'The Modern System of the Arts: A Study in the History of Aesthetics (II)', *Journal of the History of Ideas*, 13 (1952), 17–46.

LAIDLER, DAVID, 'Jevons on Money', *Manchester School*, 50 (1982), 326–53.

LANDOW, GEORGE P., *The Aesthetic and Critical Theories of John Ruskin* (Princeton, NJ, 1971).

LARSON, M. S., *The Rise of Professionalism: A Sociological Analysis* (London, 1970).

LECKY, W. E. H., *History of the Rise and Influence of the Spirit of Rationalism in Europe* (3 vols., London, 1865).

LEE, VERNON [PAGET, VIOLET], *Juvenilia* (2 vols., London, 1887).

LESLIE, CLIFFE, *Essays in Philosophy* (London, 1876).

LEVINE, PHILIPPA, *The Amateur and the Professional: Antiquarians, Historians and Archaeologists in Victorian England 1838–1886* (Cambridge, 1986).

LEWES, G. H., *The Study of Psychology* (London, 1879).

LUSCOMBE, A. M., and NEWNHAM, F. J., *The Republic of Plato* (London, 1886).

MALONEY, JOHN, *Marshall: Orthodoxy and the Professionalisation of Economics* (Cambridge, 1985).

MANDELBAUM, MAURICE, *History, Man and Reason: A Study in Nineteenth Century Thought* (Baltimore, 1971).

MARGOLIS, JOSEPH (ed.), *Philosophy looks at the Arts* (New York, 1962).

MARSHALL, HENRY RUTGERS, 'Hedonic Aesthetics', *Mind*, NS 2 (1893), 15–41.

—— *Pain, Pleasure and Aesthetics* (London, 1894).

MAYER, HANS, *Outsiders: A Study in Life and Letters*, tr. Dennis M. Sweet (Cambridge, Mass., 1982).

MILL, JAMES, *Analysis of the Phenomena of the Human Mind* (2 vols., London, 1829).

MILL, JOHN STUART, *The Collected Works of John Stuart Mill, Autobiography and Literary Essays* (ed.) John M. Robson and Jack Stillinger (London, 1981).

—— *The Earlier Letters of John Stuart Mill 1812–1848* (ed.) Francis E. Mineka (London, 1963).

MILLER, KARL, *Doubles* (Oxford, 1985).

MILLERSON, G., *The Qualifying Associations: A Study in Professionalization* (London, 1964).

MILNE, A. T., 'History and the Universities: Then and Now', *History*, 59 (1974), 33–46.

MUELLER, CARL OTFRIED, *Geschichten Hellenischer Stamme und Städte* (3 vols., Breslau, 1820–4).

NEWBOLT, HENRY, *My World as in My Time* (London, 1932).

NIEBUHR, B. G., *Lectures on Roman History*, tr. H. M. Chepmell and F. C. Demmler (3 vols., London, 1855).

PATER, WALTER, *Studies in the History of the Renaissance* (London, 1873).

—— *Marius the Epicurean*, (ed.) Ian Small (1885; Oxford, 1986).

—— *Plato and Platonism* (1893; London, 1910).

—— *The Renaissance: Studies in Art and Poetry*, (ed.) Donald Hill (1893; Berkeley and Los Angeles, Calif., 1980).

PATRICK, G. T. W., tr., *Fragments of the Work of Heraclitus . . . on Nature: Translated from the Greek Text of Bywater* (Baltimore, 1889).

PATTEN, ROBERT L., '"The People have set Literature free": The Professionalization of Letters in Nineteenth-Century England', *Review*, 9 (1987), 1–34.

PETERS, R. S. (ed.), *Brett's History of Psychology* (London, 1953).

PINKNEY, TONY, 'Lice and Literature: On Churton Collins', *News from Nowhere*, 3 (1987), 34–9.

POLLOCK, FREDERICK, 'Marcus Aurelius and Stoic Philosophy', *Mind*, 4 (1879), 47–68.

POWELL, G. H., *Plato's Defence of Socrates* (London, 1882).

PURVES, JOHN (ed.), *Selections from Plato* (London, 1883).

READER, W. J., *Professional Men: The Rise of the Professional Classes in Nineteenth-Century England* (London, 1966).

REMENYI, JOSEPH V., 'Core Demi-Core Interaction: Toward a General Theory of Disciplinary and Subdisciplinary Growth,' *History of Political Economy*, 11 (1979), 30–63.

RICKS, CHRISTOPHER, 'Arnold, Pater and Misquotation', *TLS*, 3948 (25 Nov. 1977), 1383–5.

ROACH, J. P. C., 'Victorian Universities and the National Intelligentsia', *Victorian Studies*, 2 (1959), 131–50.

ROBBINS, LIONEL, 'The Place of Jevons in the History of Economic Thought', *Manchester School*, 50 (1982), 310–25.

RORTY, RICHARD, 'The Historiography of Philosophy: Four Genres', in Richard Rorty, J. B. Schneewind, and Quentin Skinner (eds.), *Philosophy in History* (Cambridge, 1984).

ROTHBLATT, SHELDON, *The Revolution of the Dons* (London, 1968).

—— *Tradition and Change in English Liberal Education* (London, 1976).

RUSKIN, JOHN, *The Works of John Ruskin*, (ed.) E. T. Cook and Alexander Wedderburn (39 vols., London 1903–12).

ST AUBYN, GILES, *A Victorian Eminence: The Life and Works of Henry Buckle* (London, 1958).

SAMUELS, WARREN J., 'The History of Economic Thought as Intellectual History', *History of Political Economy*, 6 (1974), 305–23.

SCHILLER, FRIEDRICH, *On the Aesthetic Education of Man*, tr. Elizabeth M. Wilkinson and L. A. Willoughby (Oxford, 1967).

SEELEY, J. F., 'Elementary Principles in Art', *Macmillan's Magazine*, 16 (1867), 1–12.

SEILER, R. M. (ed.), *Walter Pater: The Critical Heritage* (London, 1980).

SHAIRP, JOHN CAMPBELL, 'English Poets and Oxford Critics', *Quarterly Review*, 153 (1882), 431–63.

SHUTER, WILLIAM F., 'Pater's Reshuffled Text', *Nineteenth Century Literature*, 31 (1989), 500–25.

SIDGWICK, ARTHUR, *Easy Selections from the Dialogues of Plato*, (London, 1888).

SMALL, IAN, 'Plato and Pater: Fin-de-Siècle Aesthetics', *British Journal of Aesthetics*, 12 (1972), 369–83.

—— 'Vernon Lee, Association and "Impressionist" Criticism', *British Journal of Aesthetics*, 17 (1977), 178–84.

—— 'Semiotics and Oscar Wilde's Accounts of Art', *British Journal of Aesthetics*, 25 (1985), 50–6.

—— 'Annotating "Hard" Nineteenth Century Novels', *Essays in Criticism*, 36 (1986), 281–93.

—— '*Marius the Epicurean* and the *Historia Augusta*', *Notes and Queries*, 34 (1987), 48–50.

—— 'Editing Pater', *English Literature in Transition*, 30 (1987), 213–18.

—— and GUY, JOSEPHINE, 'English in Crisis?', *Essays in Criticism*, 39 (1989), 185–95.

SPENCER, HERBERT, *Principles of Psychology* (2 vols., 1855; 3rd edn., London, 1881).

—— *Principles of Sociology* (London, 1876–96).

SPERBER, DAN, *Rethinking Symbolism*, tr. Alice L. Morton (Cambridge, 1975).

SPIEGEL, HENRY, *The Growth of Economic Thought* (Englewood Cliffs, NJ, 1971).

STIGLER, STEPHEN M., 'Jevons as Statistician', *Manchester School*, 50 (1982), 354–65.

STORY, W. W., 'A Conversation with Marcus Aurelius', *Fortnightly Review*, NS 13 (1873), 178–96.

STUBBS, WILLIAM, *Seventeen Lectures and Addresses on the Study of Medieval and Modern History and Kindred Subjects* (1886; 3rd edn., Oxford, 1900).

SULLY, JAMES, 'The Aesthetics of Human Character', *Fortnightly Review*, NS 9 (1871), 505–20.

—— *Sensation and Intuition* (London, 1874).

—— 'Art and Psychology', *Mind*, 1 (1876), 467–78.

SWINBURNE, ALGERNON CHARLES, *Notes on Poems and Reviews* (London, 1866).

—— *William Blake* (London, 1868).

SYME, SIR RONALD, *Ammianus and the Historia Augusta* (Oxford, 1968).

TAYLOR, THOMAS (ed.), *The Republic of Plato* (London, 1894).

THWAITE, ANN, *Edmund Gosse: A Literary Landscape 1849–1928* (London, 1984).

TOWLE, J. A. (ed.), *The Protagoras of Plato* (London, 1889).

WALLACE, WILLIAM, *Epicureanism* (London, 1880).

WARD, JAMES, 'Psychology', *Encyclopaedia Britannica* (9th edn., Edinburgh, 1875–1901), xx. 37–85.

—— 'Psychological Principles (III)', *Mind*, 12 (1887), 46–67.

WARD, W. R., *Victorian Oxford* (London, 1965).

WELLEK, RENÉ, *A History of Modern Criticism* (London, 1965).

WELLS, G. H. (ed.), *The Euthyphro of Plato* (London, 1880).

—— *The Euthydemus of Plato* (London, 1881).

—— *The Republic of Plato* (London, 1886).

WIDDOWSON, PETER, 'Terrorism and Literary Studies', *Textual Practice*, 2 (1988), 1–21.

WILDE, OSCAR, *The Collected Works of Oscar Wilde* (ed.) Robert Ross (15 vols., London, 1908–22).

—— *Two Society Comedies*, ed. Ian Small and Russell Jackson (London, 1983).

WILDE, OSCAR, *Complete Works* (London, 1967).
—— *The Importance of Being Earnest* (ed.) Russell Jackson (1980; 2nd edn., London, 1988).
—— *Lady Windermere's Fan* (ed.) Ian Small (London, 1980).
—— *The Picture of Dorian Gray* (ed.) Isobel Murray (Oxford, 1979).
WILLIAMS, RAYMOND, *Culture and Society* (London, 1958).
WOLLHEIM, RICHARD, *Art and its Objects* (1968; 2nd edn., Cambridge, 1980).
WRIGHT, T. R., *The Religion of Humanity* (Cambridge, 1986).
YEATS, W. B., and JOHNSON, LIONEL, *Poetry and Ireland* (Dundrum, 1908).

Index